What Others Are Saying About
Change Your Life Through Travel™

"Jillian Robinson's book, *Change Your Life Through Travel*, like any perfect journey, sparkles with memorable experiences, inspirational risks and joyful, unexpected adventures. You will be unable to put down this marvelous, life-affirming book, and if you do, it will only be because you are scheduling and booking tickets for your first or next travel adventure. One of the most fabulous books I have read on the profound power of travel to transform and re-vitalize lives, *Change Your Life Through Travel* is a treasure map, leading you to forgotten or undiscovered parts of yourself. As your guide, Jillian Robinson awakens you, through sensuous, evocative writing and her own irresistible spirit of adventure, to the infinite possibilities and gifts of travel. Magical by any measure, *Change Your Life Through Travel* is energizing, uplifting and profoundly generous in spirit."

MELISSA PRITCHARD
Author of *Disappearing Ingenue* and *Late Bloomer*

"Quietly appreciative of many of the world's most intoxicating locales, Robinson's pleasure-guide to self-awareness is rich with anecdote, literary seduction and the innocence that, inevitably, makes for fine art."

DR. MICHAEL TOBIAS
Global ecologist, author & filmmaker

"Fabulous book. Too many people travel and see nothing. Too many people travel from Hilton to Hilton and think they see the world. It's about time this book is written. The only reason to travel is to change your life."

ROBERT KIYOSAKI
Author of *Rich Dad, Poor Dad* and *Retire Young, Retire Rich*

~~~

"Jillian Robinson's adventures and insights provide a wonderful primer on turning travel from merely a trip to an engaging expedition of personal fulfillment. Vacations for many simply mean an escape from routine – a break from the ordinary. Heeding Jillian's advice transcends travel escape and provides insights into finding more purpose in life and uncovering moments of clarity and valuable introspection in the journey. Read, learn and grow in the process. This book will make you feel good."

WIN HOLDEN
Publisher, *Arizona Highways Magazine*

Change Your Life Through Travel™

Inspiring Tales and Tips for Richer,
Fuller, More Adventurous Living

Jillian Robinson

Footsteps Media
Scottsdale, Arizona

Change Your Life Through Travel™

Inspiring Tales and Tips for Richer, Fuller,
More Adventurous Living

First Edition

Book Design: Peri Poloni-Gabriel, Knockout Design,
www.knockoutbooks.com

Interior Photos: Jillian Robinson

Cover and Introduction Photos: Photodisc

www.footstepsadventures.com

Copyright © 2006 by Jillian Robinson

Publisher's Cataloging-in-Publication
(Provided by Quality Books, Inc.)

Robinson, Jillian.
    Change your life through travel : inspiring tales and
tips for richer, fuller, more adventurous living /
Jillian Robinson. -- 1st ed.
    p. cm.
    Includes bibliographical references.
    LCCN 2005936454
    ISBN-13: 978-0-9770168-0-8 (trade paper)
    ISBN-10: 0-9770168-0-3 (trade paper)

    1. Self-actualization (Psychology) 2. Travel--
Psychological aspects. 3. Quality of life.   I. Title.

BF637.S4R585 2006   158
                              QBI05-600182

"*Afoot and light-hearted I take to the open road,*

Healthy, free, the world before me,

The long brown path before me leading wherever I choose.

Henceforth I ask not good-fortune,

I myself am good-fortune."

WALT WHITMAN

This book is dedicated to my mother,

Gloria Robinson,

who gave me my travel wings.

And to my father,

Bill Robinson,

who always told me I could fly.

Contents

Introduction

I HAVE ALWAYS LOVED WHAT WALT WHITMAN CALLED "the open road." I love the way it pushes me into new dimensions, propels me to take greater risks. I love the fear, the uncertainty, the obstacles, the adventures, the unknown lands, smells, sounds, friends, and sometimes lovers I have met. I love the *power* of the road; and how, as Whitman said, the road expresses me "better than I can express myself."

I have been fortunate to research and produce television documentaries in various parts of the world and often solo-adventure during my time off: black-water rafting through caves in New Zealand, trekking in the Andes, driving cattle in Wyoming. All of these experiences have shaped me, but one extended odyssey changed me more than any other.

Over a six-year period, I journeyed in the footsteps of several of my literary heroes. Along the way, I discovered that each of these writers also had been transformed by travel. They all celebrated the places they visited, immersed themselves in them, and were forever changed by them. During this quest, I also found that I liked the "me" the open road had taught me to be. I wanted to reclaim her; bring her home.

I began talking with other travelers who also had felt changed by their journeys: people I'd met on past trips, or on television productions, old friends, and friends of friends. The process of hearing their stories became like travel itself. People seemed anxious to share their experiences and to recommend others who might have explored a similar path. Ultimately, I spoke with or received stories from almost seventy contemporary travelers who had glimpsed untapped aspects of themselves while away. People who had felt empowered and enriched by journeys that had enhanced their own lives, and their relationship with the world. I began to wonder: How could we take these lessons gleaned on the road and integrate them back home so that we could live richer, fuller lives every day?

A Map to this Book:
How to Start Your Journey

All of the stories in this book explore ways in which travel has changed people's lives, and how travel, or a travel state of mind, can transform our everyday living. In this book, you will journey to many parts of the world, meet a cross-section of travelers and follow in the footsteps of legendary writers to some of their favorite places: To D.H. Lawrence's Italy, Henry Miller's Greece, Isak Dinesen's Africa, Ernest Hemingway's Cuba, Mabel Dodge Luhan's New Mexico, Ed Abbey's Arizona, and Jorge Luis Borges's Argentina. You will meet travelers from a variety of countries, backgrounds, and ages, all who have been shaped by travel.

You will explore eight central themes. As I stepped, temporarily, into the lives of historic writers and talked with modern travelers, I realized the road had taught us common lessons: how to discover greater self-esteem, take more risks, and buck convention while celebrating our individuality; how to slow down and live in the moment, and connect with the power of nature while finding our wild side; lessons about feeling sexy, stepping into our courage, and living an abundant life. Each chapter in this book focuses on one of those eight life-enriching qualities, and the section "Kindle the Spirit of Travel and Life" highlights additional qualities that travelers have experienced on their journeys.

Each chapter concludes with "Tips at a Glance." These are highlights from the "Full Collection of Tips" located at the end of the book. These suggestions provide opportunities to cultivate richer, fuller living on and off the road and they include ideas from fellow travelers and legendary writers. The "Tips Summary" is a list that you can tear out, or photocopy, to take with you on your next trip, or stash in your briefcase or purse for everyday living.

You can venture into this book several ways: You can read just the stories or tips. You can reference the "Full Collection of Tips" as you complete each chapter, or read them all at once, perhaps for a rush of inspiration before a future journey. Or you can read the book from beginning to end.

Have fun with these stories and suggestions. Some ideas will work for you. Others may not. Some may be thoughts you tuck away for later years. Let them inspire your own experimentation as well. Just as my literary heroes offered me a jumping off place to discover my own passions, I hope the tales and tips within this book will provide a springboard for you and help you to enjoy a richer life experience.

Chapter 1

Discover Greater Self-esteem

EVER SINCE READING *OUT OF AFRICA, Shadows on the Grass* and *Letters from Africa*, Karen Blixen has been a hero to me. Isak Dinesen, she called herself. I fancied that she chose this name not so much to disguise her sex as to reveal her approach to life. *Isak* in Hebrew means "the one who laughs."

I was attracted to Blixen for many reasons. She was a voyager, a pioneer, a woman who bucked convention. She owned a farm in Kenya, rode a mare named Rouge and journeyed on long safaris in the bush. Wild animals did not fear her; they wandered into her home as if it were their own.

She managed the daily business of a coffee plantation. When adversity came, she dug her hands in the soil and tilled crop. She served dinners in her home on fine china with wines decanted in crystal. She was adept with medical supplies. After mending a native boy's diseased leg, he became her cook. And, in the kitchen, they shared the silent kinship of cooking.

Karen lived in harmony with the indigenous people. They came to her when they were bitten by a snake or accidentally wounded by a gunshot. She went to them when she needed to remember the abundance of risk in life, the inevitability of loss, or the regret of routine. When the government imposed compulsory labor laws and taxed the natives heavily, she fought their case with each successive governor.

Blixen feared little. She led an ox caravan to usher supplies to British soldiers during the First World War. She camped in canvas tents near a group of Masai warriors. At night she listened to the lions growl in the tall grass under a full moon. And she loved an unattainable man, who coveted space and freedom like oxygen.

As a girl, Blixen lived in Denmark and found friends in books; characters who would become her teachers, whom she would meet in her imagination. As an adult, Blixen would write to a childhood friend: "The Danish character," she said, was like "dough without leavening. All the ingredients which supply the taste and nourishment are there, but the elements which make the dough able to change, to rise, had been left out."

Africa provided the space, freedom and splendor that Blixen had longed for in her homeland. She discovered a soul-home in Africa, and once wrote: "I have become what I was meant to be here."

Glimpsing New Possibilities

"Are you in love?" a girlfriend asked one day after I had returned from Africa. I wasn't. In fact, I had just ended a cul-de-sac infatuation that had preoccupied me for more than a year. I also had been divorced for seven years and had begun to wonder whether I would ever meet a man with whom I could share my life.

But I had Kenya.

In Africa, I had sought out the living author, Kuki Gallman, who had long ago migrated from her Italian home to Kenya, and who I imagined as a kind of modern-day Karen Blixen. I had contacted Gallman from the U.S., explaining that I was traveling to Africa to research a multi-media project on Blixen. I hoped she would agree to participate.

Literary critics, Hollywood producers, and biographers had all touted the similarities between the life experiences of Kuki Gallman and Karen Blixen. Though the European women lived in Kenya more than half a century apart, Kuki's memoir, *I Dreamed of Africa*, felt highly reminiscent of Karen's life. Also, Gallman, like Blixen, had a major motion picture based on her story. Meryl Streep had become a cinematic Blixen, and Kim Basinger was Kuki's silver-screen persona.

Gallman suggested we convene at her ranch in northern Kenya. When we met, Kuki said, "You're going to join my life for the next two days, is that alright?" *All right?* It exceeded my wildest expectations. I had thought we might spend an hour or two together. Instead, she was giving me the opportunity to experience her life for two days.

On a verandah at Gallman's one hundred thousand-acre ranch, her staff served warm puff pastries on silver platters and cold ginger ale in pewter cups. Kuki's lunch guests that day included a man from the World Wildlife Fund, a representative from the Kenya Wildlife Service, and an American member of the Black

Rhino Conservation Committee.

The men had come to discuss Kuki's rhinos. She ran one of the largest private black rhino sanctuaries in the world. An estimated five hundred black rhino remained in Kenya. Fifty of those resided on Kuki's property. She was concerned there were too many males; they were beginning to fight. Perhaps importing another female would calm the males and propagate her herd. Would her lunch guests concur? If so, at what cost?

The following day, we hurtled toward the adjacent village where Kuki would present a seminar about organic farming. (Like Karen, Kuki had developed a close relationship with her indigenous neighbors.) Villagers descended on the local Red Cross building and parked rusty bicycles with tattered seat covers against spindly tree trunks. Then they shuffled into a small classroom. The Turkana and Kikuyu farmers, most wearing worn suit jackets and faded baseball caps, sat on wooden benches in rows. Kuki conducted her presentation in Swahili and stressed that as they must cultivate maize, they should do so organically. Fertilizers damaged the land. As she talked, chickens scrambled on the tin roof, scratching, dancing; but no one looked up. Some watched her without blinking; others took notes. The men laughed at her jokes, revealing scant or scraggly teeth.

When Kuki finished, she unloaded large cartons of medical supplies. Gallon jugs of cough medicine, antihistamines, syringes, malaria tablets. Kuki's old friend, Adam, who was visiting from the U.K., wandered outside with me as Kuki unpacked the final goods.

"Kuki's so passionate about what she does," Adam said.

"She sure seems it," I replied. "She must be happy, seeing all the good she can do here."

"I don't know about happy," Adam said. "It's just what she must do. She couldn't imagine not doing it."

I completely understood. Commitment came with costs. But Kuki's sense of purpose inspired me, like Karen's had, and helped me glimpse dreams for my own life.

During my remaining time in Kenya, I also learned that I had a greater spirit of adventure than I had imagined. I was more of a risk-taker than I had known. I could experience deeper enthrallment with the natural world than I had understood. And I liked myself better, much better, than when I had left home.

Finding a Lift When You Fall

Alex, an Englishwoman who now resides in America, wrote: "When I was fifty-three my life came tumbling down around me. My husband committed suicide. I was in a car accident. I had some medical problems. My children left home, and my new lover dumped me. I went into a clinical depression."

Alex had always prided herself on being "the kind of person who will have a go at anything." Coming from an "uptight" British family, she had married young the first time, into a "great, rollicking family where it was nothing to have sixteen to twenty people sit down to the dinner table. And I thought *this* is the way life should be led."

When Alex's first husband died of a brain tumor four months after they married she decided, from then on, "I was never going to waste time," she said. "I was going to do anything that cropped up. Take any opportunity that presented itself."

Yet, at fifty-three, she had lost much of this zeal.

Alex also had told me earlier, "I'm not really a very good loner. I was an only child, and didn't like being an only child. I always like to have companions when I travel."

So, a few months after life had come tumbling down around her, and while she was "still very depressed," Alex went on a journey. "I met a man who asked me if I would like to go to New Zealand with him," Alex recalled. "I quickly decided 'Why not?' And we went as 'Wwoofers.' That is, 'Willing Workers On Organic Farms.' Wwoofers are usually students, who stay with the family and work for their board and lodging. In our case, the family was expecting two young husky men, and we turn up, one man and a woman, and a middle-aged woman with arthritis at that."

Despite this, Alex recalled some "quite extraordinary" experiences while she was there. "I went damson picking," she said. "They're like very small plums you make pies and jams with. And in this area they had Maori pigs. I was told they were really gentle, but they looked fierce. I would climb my ladder to pick the damsons and, at the bottom of my ladder, would be this great sea of bristly pigs. And I drove an old diaper van into town — it had 'The Happy Nappy' written on the side — and I collected old food from the food shops; leftover pizza, cakes, fish n' chips. Then I'd feed it to the ducks and chickens back at the farm. I'd also collect eggs. I'd go on my hands and knees into these chicken coops, and I'd crawl in and slide my arm down under a chicken — and it felt lovely, so soft and downy. I also had to muck out the chicken coops."

This experience made a lasting impression on Alex. "You know when you're depressed and you don't have much energy?" she said. "You're not interested in anything. Nothing's fun. Well, doing all this was a *turnaround*. Things were *fun* again. Everything was *fascinating*, even crawling into chicken coops. And I thought *this* is what life is all about. This feels like living life to the fullest."

Alex then also quickly realized that she and her travel companion were extremely incompatible, and that she could not travel with him any longer. So, she broke a pattern. "I branched off on my own," she said. "I went by bus and train and stayed at hostels or cheap hotels. I was lonely at times, but I realized *I can do it*. And the black cloud I had been living in finally lifted. I like to think that the experience of doing something challenging and entirely on my own was the stimulation I needed to get better."

And Alex's adventures did not end there. "After I returned, I did temporary work so I could earn enough money to do more fun, exciting travels," she said. "I also had the freedom that, whenever an opportunity came up, I could do it; as long as I had enough money. I went on other adventurous trips. I went on safari in Kenya and Tanzania, and went trekking in the Himalayas." Alex also continued to branch out on her own. "I even found myself scrubbing an elephant in the shallow part of a river in the jungle at one stage," she said. "And, again, I had the feeling of *I can do it*."

Alex eventually re-married, to a man she describes as "absolutely averse to risk." Yet her husband actively encourages the quality in Alex. "He loves to live vicariously through my risk-taking," she said. And now Alex also is writing about her adventures.

Discovering Confidence
That You Didn't Know You Had ✍

Jack Dykinga is a photographer whose life also has been changed by travel. Dykinga had won a Pulitzer Prize for photographs he had made of an institution for the mentally challenged in Chicago and had developed a successful career as a staff photographer for *The Chicago Tribune*, the *Sun-Times* and, later, as photo editor for the *Tribune*. When Dykinga traveled west on a year-long leave of absence, he was quickly seduced by the power of the southwestern landscape. He relocated four years later to reside there permanently, and now devotes his career to documenting the environment through large-format photography. A pursuit he described in our public television documentary as perhaps not as "sexy" and "harder to sell to people" (than news photography) but, in the end, he believed "the most important, the most critical."

"So that is why I do what I do," he said. "That is why I have taken this 'vow of poverty,' " he kidded.

I had traveled to the Grand Canyon to produce a television program and companion web site on Dykinga. He had let my TV/web team tag along as he led an *Arizona Highways Magazine* workshop down the Colorado River. A group of amateur photographers — doctors, lawyers, retired businessmen and dot-com entrepreneurs — had joined the trip to learn at the master's side.

I remembered one participant in particular. Jim, a man in his late fifties, seemed very good-hearted, yet anxious, ill at ease, particularly at the onset of our expedition. Yet, Jim seemed to change during our week-long river-rafting journey, but I couldn't pinpoint how.

Toward the end of our trip he and I stood together, toes dipped in the river, watching the last moments of what photographers call "magic hour." The walls of the canyon shone with layers of peach, gold, mauve, and rose, as if they had been painted on the pale blue sky. In the river, a rapid swirled, the water whipping up a white whirl, like thick brushstrokes on a canvas. Jim spoke of his life back home and his initial apprehensions about this trip. Later, he expounded on his experience in a letter:

"Prior to this adventure, I had taken several photo workshops with *Arizona Highways* affiliate, Friends of Arizona Highways," Jim wrote. "We had always stayed at hotels and ventured out during the day for our pictures, returning for a warm bath in the evening.

"In the case of the rafting trip, I had a great deal of uncertainty, my anxiousness growing as the start date grew closer. I had originally enrolled because of the lead photographer's reputation. I did not pay much attention to the trip details. I figured we would probably stay at make-shift mini-motels scattered up and down the Colorado River.

"Then I started receiving more accurate descriptions in the mail, telling me what to expect. We would be sleeping outdoors every night, with no running water, bathrooms, etc. We were advised to bring special allergy medication if we were allergic to scorpions, bugs, etc. Communications with the outside world would happen only if there were an emergency; cell phones do not work at the bottom of the Grand Canyon. That's when I started asking myself what had I gotten myself into, because I am basically a couch potato.

"On the trip, photo excursions were strictly on foot. Not being an experienced hiker, I was definitely uneasy, slipping a number of times. Fortunately, my fellow photographers were very helpful, carrying my camera bag or walking/talking me down steep embankments.

"And for the first few nights, I assembled my sleeping tent, fearful of night creatures, i.e., snakes and scorpions. Assembling and disassembling the tent became pretty onerous and, about the fourth night, I was ready to take my chances sleeping under the stars. With virtually no lights in the camp, the sight of the stars was magnificent.

"By the fourth day, I felt far more comfortable with the situation. Also, I realized I could cope with the outdoors and live outside my comfort zone. It was a challenge for someone with little outdoor living experience, but I was beginning to feel that I was able to manage the situation. In short, my self-confidence increased. And I was able to enjoy the fruits of the workshop; that is, looking for splendid vistas, photographing them, and sharing ideas with my fellow photographers.

"During the first part of the trip, I was having some regrets about the timing of the workshop because I had taken the Arizona Bar Exam a few months previously. The results were supposed to be mailed the day after I started the tour and there was no way anyone could notify me during the entire trip! All I knew was that the results were awaiting my return; that the envelope would be sitting on my kitchen counter. Would the envelope's contents mean that I could practice law? That I would have to take the exam again? Or, simply, pursue another career?

"Some days I felt more confident about the envelope's contents than others. Some days I felt confident enough in myself that it didn't matter what the envelope revealed. Whatever the challenge, bring it on! I think going outside my comfort zone and beating a challenge has impacted me positively, even today," Jim concluded. "It is something no one can take from me."

Paving a Path to Your Future

David, a partner in a marketing firm and the father of two children, said, "I have been a free and independent traveler since I was fourteen years old. My first big trip was when I hitchhiked to Vegas from Chicago, by myself. After that I went to Mexico with a friend when I was sixteen. So, when I got into college, I was making money, and finally had a couple grand to fulfill a lifetime dream: to go to Europe. Decided to go alone because that was the way to go."

David bought a Eurail pass and traveled through the continent for two-and-a-half months. During his sojourn, President Nixon resigned. And David was able to gain important insights into what various Europeans thought of America during that tumultuous time.

He made several subsequent trips to Europe, and had more "on-the-ground" experiences. "I've never begged," David said, "but I've worked for my dinner. In Greece, I fished with the people on their boats."

One particularly memorable experience came two years after his first European odyssey. "A friend and I restored an old car in Luxembourg, and put twenty thousand kilometers on the car in ninety days," he said.

"We were on a shoestring budget. So we went to a junkyard and basically put a car together, repaired the car on the road when we needed to. We spent a lot of nights in junkyards all over Europe. We spent four days in Paris looking for pistons in a thirty-foot pile of pistons. Couldn't speak a word of French. They didn't speak a word of English.

"We had sleeping bags and ponchos. We didn't even have a tent. In those days, they didn't care where you slept. I slept on a parkway in Barcelona. We didn't have any cooking gear. We had a box of tools, a jack, and some circuit backs. So, as we progressed across Europe in this little Opal car, we started taking on the accoutrements of each country. In northern Europe, we bought camping gear because they have great camping gear there: tent, stove. Big beer steins for coffee mugs in Germany. Kerosene lanterns from Greece. Coffee pots from Turkey. Sleeping on hammocks and rugs that we bought in Hungary. So, pretty soon, it's not really a car, it's a caravan!

"And so, wherever we were, that's where we were," David said. "I remember nearly one hundred nights looking into the stars," he recalled fondly.

It was a great adventure for David and his companion, but there also was a more serious side, which David has never forgotten.

"Our goal was to drive to Israel," he said. "We drove all the way through Turkey.

"At the Syrian border they turned us back. They said, 'You can't go to Israel.' Israel had not yet settled things with Syria from the '73 Yom Kippur War. So they put us on a ferry and sent us to Cyprus. And, at that time, the Greek-Cypriot War was going on. Earlier that summer, on the way south out of Europe, we came streaming out of Austria and Germany on our way to see Israel, and drove right into the Turks and Greeks also leaving Western Europe to head back home and fight the Greek-Cypriot War. Drove right into it! And they weren't refugees. They were going home to kill each other."

Even today the impact remains sharp for David. "It was pretty weird for a kid," he said. "A kid out of the Midwest. I didn't even read newspapers in those days, as a young college kid. The only violence I was acquainted with was through novels — and these guys had guns."

But David's travels would serve him well. He would later go on to become the marketing head of a worldwide organization, with twelve hundred people from around the world reporting to him. "These travel experiences helped me tremendously," David said. "Not so much that I had all the answers. No. I understood the people. I could see it from their perspective. Because I had eaten with them. I had traveled on their buses with them. I could put myself in another person's shoes."

David also attributed some of his success to a humility he accrued on the road. "I was in Europe when we were at one of our lowest points [during Nixon's impeachment]. And I listened, quietly, to what people really thought about us. I've never ridden on any high horse again," he said. "And that's had a lot to do with learning humility and gaining the respect I have for other countries."

Ultimately, the road would give David one other gift he would always carry with him, and share with his children. "I can go anywhere in the world with complete confidence that I am going to be okay," he said. "Drop me anywhere, and I'll be fine. It doesn't matter what age you are, I think it's really important to be cut off from everything you know. Because it's going to go one of two ways: either you become uncomfortable, or you become comfortable. And you rise to the occasion. And, to me, that's an essential life lesson."

TIPS AT-A-GLANCE:

Discover Greater Self-esteem

1. *Seek someone you admire:* a historic or contemporary figure. Then design your own Footsteps Adventure. As you follow in their path, ask yourself what you can learn from this person and their place.

2. *Choose one quality you want more of in your life.* Then plan one activity on your next trip to foster its development.

3. *Enjoy a year of passionate living.* Devote each month of the year to developing a quality that promotes your more-passionate life: Buck Convention, Take More Risks, Slow Down and Live in the Moment...

Chapter 2

Take More Risks

NICKNAMED THE "RIVER HORSE," hippos are responsible for more human deaths in the African bush than any other animal. Before departing for Kenya I had read that an adult male can weigh more than seven thousand pounds yet can run with great velocity. Their large canine and incisor teeth, housed in a massive jaw, are their most powerful asset. Highly communal, hippo pod numbers range from two to one hundred and fifty.

In Kenya's Tsavo National Park, a lone hippo stood forty feet from the pod, grazing in shallow water. It looked different than the others. Its dual-tone skin was shiny, purplish-gray with a bib of dusty pink. Like a human afflicted with vitiligo.

I stood to pose for a photograph in front of the idle pod. A friend framed the photo, as others in our walking group resumed their trek across the hot sand. When we turned to leave, the lone hippo yawned, trumpeting his huge incisors: a demonstration that he was ready to fight.

I pulled my camera snug to my face and peered through it. Beneath the hippo's pocked, tar-colored snout, a fleshy, cavernous throat widened, threatened. I stared into the hippo's eyes, unwavering: as if to say, "I dare you."

I was not at all proud of this response.

The hippo issued several long, continuous barks. Our group continued strolling and the massive animal bolted straight toward us.

"Move it!" our trekking leader, Makau, yelled.

The group began to run. I froze, hoping to get one final photograph.

The hippo's tubby, hulking body hurtled from squat, stumpy legs. He smashed and tossed water in his wake. I watched him approach, and clicked my camera shutter, twice.

One of the guards stepped in front of me and cocked his gun; the rifle pressed firm against his cheek. I had never before heard a gun cocked, except in the movies. It is a sound I never want to hear again.

Before the guard, the hippo stopped running. Beads of water dropped from the mammal's hide. Several long strands dangled from his jaw, like rain falling from an awning during a summer storm. The hippo stood, motionless, staring at us. I looked back at him, now ashamed of whatever role I had played in provoking his response.

I trotted on to join the others; then walked, in startled silence, feeling guilty and shaky from the encounter. *What was this strange compunction to court peril?* - I wondered. *Dance with danger. Fly close to the flame.* I had always felt like mostly a "good girl," who followed rules diligently and did not seek unnecessary risks. Yet, as I strolled again across Tsavo's hot, open sands, I began to wonder: *Where else in my life might I take unimagined risks?*

The Faces of Risk ✐

Ernest Hemingway was a consummate risk-taker. He hunted lions in Africa. Fought in amateur bullfighting contests in Spain. Deep-sea fished in Havana and Florida. Chased U-boats in Cuba. Served as a correspondent in World War II. Hemingway thrived on risks, and his life became a legend because of it. Hemingway also seemed so *alive* because of his risk-taking: as if his life were more fully lived because he embraced the spirit of adventure.

But our risks don't have to involve battling bulls or fighting marlin. They can be gentler risks, *quieter.* Like the first time you told someone you loved them —- or the last time. Or when you asked your boss for a raise or a promotion. These moments still may feel risky, even if we have experienced them many times before.

Risk suggests possible loss or danger. And fear of loss often preoccupies our lives. What if we *embraced* loss instead? What if we regarded every possible loss as an opportunity to create something new? Doors close, windows open.

In Jorge Luis Borges's Buenos Aires I learned not about Hemingway-esque dares, but about everyday risks. In many ways, Borges was antithetical to Hemingway: bookish, preferring his adventures closer to home. Yet it was in Borges's footsteps that I discovered about *quiet* risks that can lead to magic moments.

Learning to See Differently

I had not considered taking my own Footsteps Adventure when I planned my trip to Argentina. I was going to fulfill a longtime dream: to dance the tango in Buenos Aires. Yet, as with most good journeys, I discovered so much more while making other plans.

Three weeks before my departure, the general manager of the PBS station where I worked plopped into the pea green chair in my office and asked where I was traveling to next. I told him Buenos Aires, and he asked if I had read Borges. I told him I hadn't. He continued gulping down the Girl Scout cookies I had placed on my desk as he hop-scotched topics from new productions I had in development to stock market tips to dog breeding and international travel. But before he left, he enigmatically said, "You should read Borges," and disappeared.

In the following three weeks I learned that Borges was a great traveler — in his own backyard. Born in Argentina in 1899, Borges's family moved to Europe when he was a teenager. He later returned to South America and realized his destiny was to write of his homeland.

"Borges had had an insatiable appetite for the streets of Buenos Aires," biographer James Woodall wrote. He walked everywhere. Through alleys lined with pastel-colored homes in La Boca, past colonial buildings in the neighborhood of San Telmo, and down the humble streets in outlying districts.

These explorations also became a journey to his heart. "Uncovering layers, some real, some imagined, of his home city, he found aspects of himself that might have remained buried had his family stayed in Europe," Woodall said. In Buenos Aires, Borges penned works such as *Doctor Brodie's Report, El Aleph,* and *Ficciones,* and literally hundreds of essays and poems inspired by his native country.

During my quick study, I also uncovered three details about Borges that, ultimately, would shape my journey: Borges was blind, he was passionate about tango, and he was obsessed with Walt Whitman, my favorite American poet.

I also learned that Borges was a risk-taker: He dared political dissension almost his entire life. He bucked literary conventions in fiction. And he spent most of his adulthood in love, though it was almost always unrequited.

I liked this about Borges. It kindled in me a flame for him as I ventured into his homeland.

Early in my Buenos Aires sojourn, I was invited to the home of Perez Celis. He and his wife, Iris, were friends of friends and had asked me to join them for dinner. Celis, I would later learn, is one of Argentina's most famous artists. That evening they also hosted a group of blind painters, who had come to show Celis their work, and to drink and converse.

When Iris had first asked me to join their group, I hesitated. I had come to Argentina to dance. I felt a bit awkward, too. I was not an artist. I was not blind. I only spoke high-school Spanish. How could I contribute?

After a hot shower, I chastised myself. Travel was about such experimentation, dangling toes in untested waters. I reminded myself that Borges had been blind. Perhaps this would be an interesting evening.

As I rode in a cab to Celis's home, I wondered, *What else had I missed by choosing the comfort of the familiar? What other opportunities had eluded me because I saw only through a certain lens?*

Where else had I been blind?

At the home of Celis and Iris, Iris showed me a collection of Celis's completed work. Then she guided me through a series of paintings Celis was currently creating; an ode to one of *his* literary heroes, Walt Whitman.

Then a blind man showed me how to dance.

One of the men from the group awaited Iris and me at the stairwell. He showed me his colleagues' paintings stacked against Celis's wall. I marveled at their work. How was it possible to paint so vividly without sight? I finally summoned the courage to ask my guide.

He grabbed my hand and led me to the drafting table. He began to sketch in silence. He paused, ran his fingers across the grained paper and continued drawing. He pursued this rhythm of sketching then stroking until a finely-formed landscape breathed from the once-lifeless pad.

Later that evening, as I strolled the last few blocks to the Amagro dance club, I thought again of the blind man. His work is how tango should be: with cheeks pressed together, we are denied the usual gaze. Only our bodies can guide us from the darkness. We must feel, not think.

And when I danced that night, I experienced a sensation I had never known before.

Strains of Pugliese seeped through the speakers. The tango music was charged, electric. My partner, a man I had met one dance before, pressed his moist, warm cheek next to mine. I felt his breath against my skin and smelled traces of Old Spice on his neck. I laced my arm over his shoulder and he nuzzled into me.

I closed my eyes and followed his lead. My body pulsed as I waited for each consecutive move. His leg surged forward; mine lunged back, mirroring his. He created space for me to play. I slithered my foot up the back of his calf — shining my shoe, baiting our flirtation. He spread his legs. I slid my foot across the floor as if striking a match and flicked my leg back between his: a bold *gancho*. He returned the gesture. We continued back and forth like this, a single body with four legs.

For a moment, I was in love: with the music; with this embrace; with the current that bound us; with this communication that needed no words, with this moment. This "tango moment," my American dance friends would later tell me.

Quiet risks are like dancing the tango: suffused with subtle whispers, silent invitation, soft nudges, and sweet surrender.

Travel often provides such opportunities to venture, gently, into the unknown. How many more enriching experiences could we have in our lives, if only we saw through a different lens?

Now, whenever I feel daunted by a new opportunity, I always try to take it. Because I know that down that road is often where the magic moments lie.

Becoming a Kid Again

Kate, an artist, told me, "As a kid, I was fascinated with Nancy

Drew and Sherlock Holmes," she said. "I was a voracious reader. I'd hide in the attic with a bag of apples and a stack of books. And in high school, my mother would say, 'Why don't you go out on a date? You're always home reading.' "

Kate encountered Captain Cook and other literary inspirations in this cloistered attic. "I read Jane Eyre when I was eleven. I read that book twice. I just knew that I was going to see everything and do everything," she said. And these books helped nourish Kate's dream of "leaving home and exploring more of the world," someday.

But it wasn't always an easy path to these new horizons.

"When I was in second grade, I asked my parents for art lessons. They said, 'Okay, we can take you to the museum for classes, but you're going to have to take the bus home.'

"So, my father drives me downtown, shows me where I'm supposed to get off the bus in downtown Syracuse, change buses and transfer. *I'm in second grade.*

"So, from a second grader's point of view, up on a bus looking down, I don't know where to get off. I don't know where to make my transfer, because everything downtown looks the same. So I finally decide I better get off the bus. I stand there for a half an hour, looking for the right bus. And I'm not worried. I figure something's going to happen. And, sure enough, a bus comes by and I recognize the street name on the front of the bus because it's near my school. So I hop on, handle the transfer, get off at my school, and walk home, three hours late.

"My parents are frantic. And I'm thinking, *I did it! I found my way home! It was rough, but I did it!* And they were freaking out.

They made me feel like I had failed.

"It took me a while to get over that fear of failure in traveling because I think it set a little travel anxiety in my mind of *You can't do this. No. Stop.*"

But this did not prevent Kate from harboring more travel dreams.

"One of the most important papers I ever did was 'Life on a Coral Reef' in seventh grade," she said. "So my dream was always to go to the Great Barrier Reef. And then, as an adult, I finally made it there! It was big for me to make that connection after all those years.

"There was a trail that led to a beach where Captain Cook landed; and these enormous spider webs. Enormous. The spiders were two inches in body size. They were all over the place. And I felt this squeamishness about crocodiles and big spiders.

"So it was going to be a matter of transcending the terror of what else was along that path to get to that beach where he landed. And no one was around, and it looked very spooky and dangerous. But I just sucked it up and said, 'You know, if the trail's here someone's done it before me. And nothing's stopping me from getting to that beach.'

"It wasn't a big risk," Kate added. "It was a quiet risk. And it was the fantasy of being some kind of explorer. It was fun."

And when Kate reached the beach, she said, "It was gorgeous. Perfect… Just perfect."

Kate later told me, "I think of travel as play and adventure."

And she keeps this spirit of travel alive back home. "One thing I've done is I've set a goal of hiking every mile of all seven mountain preserves in the Phoenix Mountain Preserve system. That forces me to get out of my regular hikes. I also get out into these spaces and I feel like I'm eleven years old again!" she said. "I'm a tomboy and I'm having an adventure. I've never been on this trail before. I'm not sure where it's going. I may have a map. But I'm going to have to find my way back," she said. "It's that rush you get. I'm on this trail. I'm not so sure where I am. It feels so good. It's so beautiful. It's so exciting. Let's see where we end up."

As Kate spoke, I realized, it is like the spirit of dance, and so many other adventures we might have in our lives. If we could just always say, "I'm not sure where I am. It's so exciting. Let's see where we end up." As we once had, when we were kids.

Finding Magic and New Focus ✒

Renee, a writer in her forties and mother of two, said, "I grew up traveling; travel the great teacher, pinnacle of all learning experiences. And I guess, for me, there had to be an element of danger. Life in the raw, on the edge, informed my soul: It changes who I am and tells who I am at the same time."

Like Kate, Renee also glimpsed her future travels through books. "As a kid, I read about a teacher who went to Alaska," she said. "She'd planned to spend a year there, but married into a village and wound up staying. It was a very simple book, but I was just fascinated by it because she was very young and just going there changed her whole life."

Renee then followed the teacher's path. In her twenties, she traveled to the bush in Alaska to teach mentally-challenged children and met with her own adventures.

"One day, there was a man who came to the next village on a homebuilt raft," Renee said. "I was fascinated by this little Huck Finn raft and knew I had to hop on. A woman got off the raft, saying, 'I'm not getting on that raft again. I'm not going near that man. I'm out of here!' What did I do? I was smart enough to go with another teacher, but we climbed on and went downstream with this man.

"It was an amazing little raft," Renee said. "He'd built it out of junk. He was kind of a junk man, and that was the part that fascinated me: that anyone that could take bits of motors and pieces of washing machines and make this thing run.

"It was actually two rafts put together; it had two half houses on each side. And he had a little skiff. And that skiff slotted between these two half bunkhouses. And he could take it out and go plant the raft somewhere.

"He also had the inside of a washer tub that he used as a fish corral, down underneath the boat. And he would catch salmon as he floated down the river so he would have a constant source of food. And he had old tire rims and a grate over that, and he would grill fish on the grate going down the river.

"In the wintertime, he would disassemble it, putting the two houses together to make one little house out of them. The thing came together and apart like it was engineered.

"Well, I jumped on that raft. I thought that this was the most fascinating thing I'd ever seen. And we took a day trip. We went down on the Yukon River. Then we came back up at sunset. It was just one of those halcyon moments. You know: this is how life is meant to be.

"Then, all of the sudden, the motor started making a different noise. We had sheared a pin in the motor. It was an antique motor, probably no more than three horsepower. So, we were stuck. We had to spend the night. And, in September on the Yukon, it gets below freezing.

"I don't remember being scared. I never questioned," she said. "And I could have easily avoided all of that. The rule of growing up is 'Don't go home with strangers.' But there were so many other times in my travels where it had opened up this beautiful world...

"People throughout my life have said that I am a good, quick judge of people. And I think it comes from dancing on that edge," she said. "It's those quick reads. And having a series of baseline experiences where you know how to trust yourself."

Renee's willingness to take risks and follow her intuition enabled her to enjoy another "halcyon moment," and apply another important lesson she had learned.

"It's just always a matter of focusing on what you're doing next," Renee said. "One thing I learned in Alaska was that people who lived there a long time were not as spontaneous as we are in the Lower 48. You planned carefully and thought things through for where you were going. I had stuffed my pockets full of dried fish and candy bars. And he had some water on the boat. So that saved us for that day."

The trio did not need to spend more nights on the Yukon either. "We got really lucky. Come Sunday night, when two of the five teachers were missing, they started looking," she said, "and found us."

On the afternoon that I interviewed Renee she mentioned that she was battling cancer. She apologized, in advance, if she wasn't as sharp as usual. She'd had surgery forty-eight hours earlier, had just come from the doctor's office, and was on powerful pain medication. Yet she kept this interview with me, practically a stranger. Clearly, Renee's lesson of "focusing on what you're doing next" still applied in her life today.

"When I think of the cancer, my husband always says, 'You're so brave,' " Renee told me. "And I've said, 'You know, it's just a matter of focusing forward. If you look at the next step and move through it, the power that would've gone into being afraid kind of carries you through, and pushes you forward; because you know there's more after this.' "

Weeks after our interview, I re-read a note that Renee had written me before our talk. I realized that she had learned another important lesson from her travels: how to savor the memories back home. And I thought how looking forward, as well as backward, could help us *all* to remember in difficult times: "There's more after this."

As Renee wrote:

"For twenty-five years or more, I have always carried home with me a stone from my travels. They collect — continents colliding in a glass jar under a window — a reminder of the places I've been, the people I've met.

"I watch the people, follow them to their homes. Watch what they cook. How they cook it. Take pictures, gather the recipes. I learned how to make German Spaetzle the Schwaebisch way from a woman in Hohenstaufen, Germany. I didn't know that my own great-grandmother made it that way until returning home.

"From Brazil, we clothed our Phoenix floors in tightly woven, colorful rugs. We brought back cassava flour and dende oil and made mochaka: a clay pot rice and shrimp dish. We take pictures, learn dance steps, write stories while we are there.

"We collect foods, music, traditional pieces of clothing, learn a tradition, a song, a poem. My brain collects/charts smells — diesel puts me in Prague, Paris, Muenchen, Budapest, on the street with the gypsies and beggars in Salvador. Until I come to and am waving at my seven year old as the fumes from the school bus cloak me in an Arizona midlife morning."

TIPS AT-A-GLANCE:

Take More Risks

1. *Add a quiet risk to your next journey.* You don't need to know what the risk is, just go with the intention that you will create one. Then at your destination allow the moment to unfold.

2. *Try one new thing each year.* Ever thought about performing stand-up comedy? Attending a relationship seminar? Learning to fly an airplane? Embrace one new activity each year that involves risk and growth.

3. *See your hometown or state through a new lens.* Whether with colleagues from work, a spouse, partner or friend, create "mystery dates" to explore a place or activity you've never experienced before.

Chapter 3

Buck Convention,
Celebrate Your Individuality

A LEX, THE ENGLISHWOMAN who traveled to New
Zealand, also mentioned in our interview, "I was Salvador
Dali's model for a little bit."

How had she managed to pose for one of the twentieth
century's greatest painters? I wanted to know.

The answer linked to her roots.

"I had a stepmother who never did anything because it was,
'What would the neighbors say?' It was an extremely boring and
tucked-up, inhibited life. And I decided very early on that that
wasn't me.

"Shortly after my father died, I gave up my job, and a girlfriend
and I went to live in Spain for the summer. We hitchhiked there
and stayed in tents we had to hold up with meat skewers," she
said. "But we always wore skirts because you had to wear skirts
in Franco's day.

"We rented this so-called 'villa' in Spain — it was a fisherman's cottage. And we made our living by having people come for sort of 'bed and breakfast.' But 'bed' was your own sleeping bag on the floor and 'breakfast' was croissants from the local baker. We were in our twenties and nobody had any money. It was very primitive, loads of fun," Alex said.

"We did this in this village called Cadaques, which is where Salvador Dali was. Technically, he was in Port Lligat, which is just a few houses over a promontory on the bay.

"And, one day, I was walking through town and a car stopped, and a man asked me the way in French and then realized that I spoke English. That led to an invitation for a drink, and he turned out to be a French nobleman, who was a sculptor and had come to the village to make an official bust of Salvador Dali. And, well, we became lovers," Alex said.

"Georges set up his studio to do this sculpture in a stable. It had a donkey on one side and the other side was empty. Salvador Dali would come every now and then and pose. And I would go and watch, and talk to Georges. And staying at this B&B we were running was a truly beautiful girl. Her name was Eve, appropriately enough, and she had this perfect oval face, and was an art student. When she heard that I knew Dali a little bit, she asked if she could come and meet him. So I asked Georges, and he said, yes, she could meet him. So she came with me one day when Dali was coming to pose. And Dali took one look at her and said, 'Oh, you are *magnificent!* You are so beautiful! I would like to paint you. You must come to my house.' And then he looked at me and said, 'Oh, you're not beautiful, but you can come and see my house too.'

"So I went as Eve's sort of handmaiden. We went to his house and he set us up in a two-story room. And he had a chair that was like a throne, with big swan wings on either side of it up on the upper half of it, and he was down below with his easel. And he said to Eve, 'Take your clothes off and go onto the stage and I'll go and put on some music.' I had never heard of music speakers. This is going back to about 1962. I hadn't heard of putting music on in one room and hearing it in another. I thought that was pretty exotic.

"So he went into another room and put on some music. And he came back, and Eve had a very athletic figure, and he said, 'Oh, but you have the figure of a boy!' And then he looked at me, and I'm a bit plump, and he said, 'You have the figure of a *woman!* Take your clothes off.' And I said, 'No, no, no. I couldn't possibly do that.' And Eve, being an art student, said, 'Don't be so silly. Of course you can.'

"So, that's how it all began. And that first day he posed us together. And then, after that, he dismissed Eve, and I went back every day for about three weeks. And he did hundreds and hundreds of sketches. He didn't really do the face at all. It was just an oval. Since then, I've seen many similar sketches, and obviously I wasn't the only girl he ever sketched. I think any young girl was pretty fair game, you know. Honored to pose for a famous artist, even if her face would remain anonymous.

"And that was my fifteen minutes of fame," Alex said, "because, for a very short time, as I walked around the town, people would say, 'That's Dali's model.' There also was a Belgian millionaire who introduced himself to me. He had a yacht in the bay and he would send his chauffeur-driven boat to pick me up for lunch on the boat. It was such a glamorous, exciting summer!" she said.

Alex quickly settled into life back home, "just as a secretary" as she called it, but she would always remember this rich, memorable departure from her British upbringing. "If I had behaved the way I should have behaved, according to my stepmother," Alex said, "when Georges asked me to have a drink with him, I should have said 'No!' And that would have been the end of it." Instead, Alex seized the spirit of adventure she had sworn to as a child and enjoyed her "fifteen minutes of fame."

Breaking the Mold
and Making a New One

"Travel does change your life," Jeanette said. "It gives you a freedom that you probably didn't know you were allowed to have. It's given me a different view of the world. If I had stayed on Long Island, in my little community, I never would have known near what I know now. I never would have met the people I have, and people of all social strata. So travel has made me grow and given me the kind of freedom that many people have never experienced." Jeanette is a native New Yorker who has lived in California, the Virgin Islands, and Arizona and has traveled to countless other places, almost always alone.

"I remember growing up, people tell you all the things you can't do. They tell you that you get married, you stay at home, you marry someone you know, and grew up with, with the same values. And lots of people do that. But I didn't," she said.

Jeanette's first move was into the military. "I did my basic training in Alabama, my medical training in Texas, went to Maryland and then, from there, to Massachusetts. So, in a short period of time, I did a lot of traveling.

"The military is what gave me my total affirmation," she continued. "It's what made me realize that I could leave home and that it would be all right. It really got me started on wanting to see other things and be free. And, when I got out of the military, I went back home and decided to drive cross-country to live in California. I packed my bags and everyone told me I was crazy because I had a little baby who was no more than six-months old. They said, 'You can't do that. Your car will never make it over the mountains.'

"But I made it and it was really liberating to get out there. Of course there was a fear because you tend to believe these people. You trust their experience because they're older and then you get out there, and actually start doing it, and you realize, *Here I am, I'm quite content, and this is a* good *thing.* Otherwise, I would have stayed in my little cubbyhole and married my high school sweetheart, and grown up exactly like my mother and he would've grown up exactly like his father, and we would've had lots of children, and we'd be telling them the same things: 'Don't go there. Don't do this.' "

Jeanette continued to venture out of her "cubbyhole" on another major expedition when "not knowing anyone down there, not knowing what to expect, I packed my bags one day and moved to the Virgin Islands," she said. She also quickly discovered that "As you go into different cultures, you have to learn to let go of some of the things that are ingrained in you. Like in the Virgin Islands, the attitude is so laid back. They have this thinking like 'everything is going to be alright.' And, being from New York, and elsewhere in the United States, we have this rush, rush, rush attitude. I'm more laid back than I've ever been in my entire life, and it's because of my experiences on the Virgin Islands," Jeanette said. "I know, no matter what happens, life is going to go on. If you do it in a rush, it's going to go on. And if you do it slowly, it's going to go on. The same things are going to happen, whether you do it in a hurry or you're doing it slowly. So you do it how it makes you feel best."

As Jeanette talked, I realized that even though we'd been friends for years I'd never asked what it was like for her, as an African American woman, to move to Phoenix.

"According to the statistics there was a two percent African American population in Phoenix when I came," she said. "And I can remember, driving down the street one day, and this very attractive black woman looked over and she started rubbing her face. We both had our windows closed and she smiled and waved and went on about her business. And I'm thinking, *Okay, there must be something on my face.* And what she was really saying to me was that it was so nice to see another black person!

"It was amazing to me that I had never thought about it, and here she was grateful to see someone else of color in Phoenix! I laughed about it when it finally dawned on me what she was trying to say," Jeanette said.

"It never crosses my mind," she continued. "When I see people, I see *people.* I don't see cultures or colors. I just see people. It's been so wonderful in my traveling that I have met people who feel the same as I do and have accepted me, as a *traveler*. I find that people who have traveled are more open to accepting differences in people. You expose yourself to a wider range of people and get to the point where you realize that people are all the same no matter where. They just do things a little differently."

At fifty-seven, still willing to travel and move to new locales, Jeanette realizes that "Once you embrace the big picture, you're not content with the little one," she said. "You also understand that you can take all of the cultures you've been to and meld them into one. I think a lot of people don't go back to their roots once they've traveled because they find that there *is* a different way of doing things; a way that they prefer," she said. "And you realize that you have *choices*."

Making a Difference Being Different

Karen Blixen, as mentioned earlier, bucked convention. She dared to be different. Biographer Judith Thurman said that, even as a child, Blixen "had a precocious confidence in her own singularity."

One of Blixen's first artistic influences, Georg Brandes, wrote: "On entering life, young people meet with various collective opinions…The more the individual has it in him to become a real personality, the more he will resist following a herd." Blixen's other early literary heroes also reflected this unconventional spirit. They were bold, charismatic characters that blazed their own paths, created their own myths. Karen found solace in these figures.

In Africa, she cultivated this lack of convention. She and her lover, Denys Finch Hatton, never married, but led what Blixen called "parallel lives." And Blixen never bore children, at a time when society clearly expected a woman would.

Karen also did not conform to the white English settler groups, with whom she debated the capabilities and rights of the native Kenyans. She lobbied for schooling for the indigenous people. She maintained that the Africans would get their country back one day, and wanted to help prepare them for that eventuality. Ultimately, Blixen would open a school on her property to teach them herself.

Discovering You Are the Same, Only Different

I would follow in Karen's footsteps to Kenya's Loita Hills, home to the most traditional-living Masai, where I would camp and walk for three days with the Masai through their land.

"How many kids you have?" Murianga, a once-Masai warrior, asked me the day after we had met. Murianga did not display his long, pierced lobes — a Masai sign of beauty — but, rather, curled them around his ear, like little piglet tails. He grinned broadly and often, unconcerned by his missing front teeth.

"None," I told him, and felt awkward. Children and cattle were the most prized possessions in Masai culture. Also, through my African journey, I had been ruminating over a dilemma that many thirty-something women faced. *Did I want to have children? If I never married again, would I consider having a child on my own? As I had been independent for so long, would I be happy trading the pleasures of travel and freedom for the promised joys of motherhood? And if I did not have children, would I feel selfish? Suffer regret later on?*

I remembered Karen. She had written in her letters, "I do not think anyone can be happy except in conditions that…they have chosen as the expression of their true nature."

She later added, "I have always believed that one could not expect to get too much out of life if one were not able to clarify for oneself what is 'essential' for one, and that when this demanded it of one to let everything else go."

For Blixen's own life she decided, "It had become quite clear to me that I did not want to have a child." And later she revealed, "I prize my freedom above everything else that I possess."

Did I, too, prize my freedom above all else? If not, was childbearing my "essential" element? What would I choose if I had to "let everything else go"?

For the next few days, I walked through the savannah with the Masai, threw their spears, hurled their clubs, sat with them in the grasses as they crafted their bows, watched a blood-letting ceremony where a prized heifer was poked in the jugular, and I was offered a taste of the sacred blood-milk.

On my final day, I visited Murianga's village and home. He sat inside his *boma* with one of his two wives and three of his children. The kids surrounded their father. Robert, a Masai man who spoke English well, sat beside them.

The *boma's* interior had one room. In the center, a fire provided warmth and light. The roof was low and smoke permeated the thatched walls. I joined the others on the dirt floor.

Robert began talking about *boma* life. I surveyed the two

bedrooms from my seat; a taut, cowhide bed filled each. Wooden poles adjoined the *boma's* main area with the animal den, where goat kids and newborn calves jostled and cried.

Murianga's children started to fidget and wander off. Murianga called them back. They reassembled around him. The son that bore his father's broad smile stood by his side. As Robert continued talking, the boy placed his small hand on his dad's shoulder. Murianga lifted him, turned him upside down and kissed him, heartily, on his cheek, as if no one else were there.

In that moment, I realized that children and cattle were the Masai's most prized possessions, yet, suddenly, I felt completely fine that I possessed none of my own similar abundance. I understood that we all shared common joys but traveled different paths to obtain them.

Finding Two Worlds

Maire, a university professor and an executive in the health-care industry, told me:

"My parents are from Estonia. I'm a first generation American. My mother fled from invading Communists, leaving her family behind with the vague notion that freedom existed somewhere beyond the Baltic Sea shoreline. My father's fate was more precarious. He was an officer in the Estonian Army, and spent a year in a German P.O.W. camp. Then the Russians inscripted him on a blacklist, and he fled in the middle of the night on a boat to Sweden. He eventually migrated to the U.S.

"My mother and brother first lived on 123rd Street in New York. Both fair-skinned, platinum blonds, they stood out as 'others' in the predominantly African American community there. For me, when girls were wearing Danskin sweaters, Buster Brown saddle shoes and Pendleton pleated skirts, my parents, of course, couldn't afford these things, working so hard to make the mortgage payment each month. So, I didn't quite fit in with the mainstream and was self-conscious of my embroidered knee socks and hand-me-down clothing.

"While my brother and I desperately tried to be American, our instincts still fought assimilation. We continued to speak Estonian at home, and I had a slightly uneasy feeling that my parents were somewhat different from our friends' parents. Sometimes they even embarrassed us in public with their thick accents," Maire said.

"Over the years, I received letters and black-and-white photographs from family in Estonia. My parents couldn't even telephone there because of my father's history. I wanted to visit, but my parents said I couldn't. I'd 'get lost' picking mushrooms there.

"My father died in 1991, one month before Estonia was freed," Maire said. "Then I decided to visit. I took my son, who was around twelve at the time. And, when we got through the glass doors at customs, there were *thirty people* waiting there for us. It was like that scene in *Pleasantville,* where everyone went from black-and-white to color.

"I felt *buoyed* by the experience," Maire said. "I came from a small family and had always felt a bit envious of others who had big families — cousins, grandparents, etc. In Estonia, everyone was saying, 'You always have a home here.' It was like the family I never had.

"I visited a cousin who still had a pull-chain toilet, and everyone in the family would take one bath a week, using water boiled from the stove. Everyone would share the same tub of water," Maire said.

"I discovered that my father's best friend was still alive, and I went to his house, where I had coffee and cake and champagne with him. He had so many stories to tell. I felt I could touch my father's past by meeting this man.

"My mother, who was now handicapped, had drawn maps for me showing where she'd grown up and lived; the cemeteries, etc. I saw all of this history and it helped me understand what they had been through. And where my roots were.

"Growing up I had always felt a bit like F. Scott Fitzgerald," Maire said. "Like an outsider looking in. I called it 'having a foot in two worlds.' That trip told me it was okay to be in both. It gave me the balance I needed."

Maire has continued to plant her feet in both worlds, and walk her own path. While maintaining a career in healthcare today, she also has taught Estonian in schools, participated in ethnic diversity festivals, and performed Estonian folk dancing in New York. Though both of Maire's parents are now deceased, she realizes that their speaking their native language at home also was her parents' "way of holding onto their culture and passing it along to us as well," she said. And, today, she and her brother still converse in the language their parents once taught them.

Buck Convention, Celebrate Your Individuality

1. *Discover what is essential to you.* Look to the road for clues. And when you find landmarks, return to them, celebrate them.

2. *Be different.* Step outside your "normal" behavior on your next journey. If you typically follow, lead for a day. Buck your own convention.

3. *Draw outside the lines.* Recall who and what you wanted to be when you were a kid, alone in your room at night. What did you do when you drew outside the lines? Consider one thing you can do tomorrow to touch, or relive, that childhood dream.

Chapter 4

Slow Down and
Live in the Moment

M ARK, AN ACCOMPLISHED, YOUNG CEO who often logs sixteen-hour days and is quick to admit to having prioritized business over romantic relationships, said, "I like how I am with myself more when I'm away."

Reflecting on a trip to the British Virgin Islands, he said, "I was present, in the moment there. I'd walk into the local cafes and talk to people; really talked, and connected with them. At home, there's never enough time. *If* I have time to call friends, it's a ten-minute talk. I'm too busy to really slow down, connect."

But in the British Virgin Islands Mark realized, "That's not enough. I want more than that," and he began meditating, for the first time in his life, on that trip.

"Since then, I've meditated every day for forty minutes before I start work. I begin my meditations by reviewing images in my head from my travels. Sitting on the beach in the British Virgin

Islands is my favorite image. But, occasionally, I go through others, like the Grand Canyon, the beauty of the view from a Colorado mountain peak or the dew in morning in Napa. And I immediately feel expanded. It reminds me how incredible this world is."

And it slows Mark down.

A month after he had returned from the British Virgin Islands, his vice president of operations said to him, "I don't know what you took, or what you did, while you were on vacation but you're different."

And Mark told me, "And you know what? I am. I have more patience with my staff. I listen better to their problems. Even in the grocery store, I stop to look the clerk in the eye to say 'Thank you.' And people seem grateful, just for my taking the time to acknowledge them."

Mastering the Art of Living in the Moment

Have you ever passed a tree you've seen countless times but never before noticed the intricate design on its bark? Or how the grass balds at a certain spot on your everyday route? Or a flowering bush, previously unnoticed, in your neighbor's yard? In the past you've most likely had other things on your mind, instead of immersing yourself in the moment.

Often we become so busy dealing with our daily lives and commitments that weariness sets in, and we no longer see, smell, taste, touch, and hear with the same purity we did when were children.

What about in your travels? Have you ever noticed several days into a vacation that you have completely forgotten about a problem that had consumed you a week earlier? Or have you taken a long weekend jaunt and felt like you had been gone for a much longer time?

I believe this sense of timelessness occurs when we slow down and live in the present, as we often are able to do while we are away, disengaged from the continuous loop that typically plays in our minds about the past or the future. This insistent refrain, ironically, can prevent us from moving forward in our lives because its din leaves us too fragmented to find our way.

D.H. Lawrence seemed to master this art of living in the moment in Italy.

The peripatetic author lived in several countries, including America, Mexico, Australia and his native Britain. Yet he always returned to Italy. He lived in Lake Garda/Gargnano, Fiascherino/Lerici, Taormina, Spotorno and Florence/Scandicci. He explored numerous Italian destinations in between.

Lawrence had a tempestuous love affair with Italy. Though he sporadically grumbled about the country, he more often delighted in it. His Italian residence totaled five years, a quarter of his creative career, and he penned three of his four travel books about the country: *Sea and Sardinia*, *Twilight in Italy* and *Etruscan Places*. He also composed *Lady Chatterley's Lover* and completed *Sons and Lovers* while living in Italy, and various short stories and poems are set there.

Italy was the place that awakened Lawrence's senses. He walked the paths of the locals. Smelled their flowers. Made friends at neighborhood pubs. Picked olives with the peasants. Produced his own wine. Browsed in local shops. Preserved figs, and made jam with his wife, Freida. He sat in his garden, watching birds, or a butterfly that would "sit content on my shoe." He savored the often-sunlit ways of the Italian people, immersed himself in their culture, settled into their rhythm. And in so doing, as his biographer Leo Hamalian said, "He found the essence of his being."

Celebrating the Senses ✍

Italy has captivated me since the age of sixteen, when I traveled to Italy with my mother, and later when I studied in Florence for a semester during college. I loved the Italians' passion for life and hoped to discover more of it. Years later, after reading and researching the experiences of D.H. Lawrence, I returned to Italy. This time, divorced for five years, I journeyed alone.

One of my stops was at a villa on a seventeenth-century estate. It was built around a thousand-year-old tower and was part of a working farm, which is why I chose it. I had never stayed on a farm and thought it sounded romantic. Also, Lawrence had reveled in farm life when he lived in Tuscany.

The Podoro estate overlooked the Arno Valley and Florence in the distance. Lawrence's house crowned a hilltop on the other side. Only seven miles outside of the city, the area was thoroughly rural and quintessentially Tuscan.

The afternoon I arrived I met Piero, the estate manager's nephew. He was a slender man with a compact frame and a salt-and-pepper beard. And when he talked, his whole body got involved.

I learned that the villa was not serving dinner that evening, so

I would need to travel into Florence to find supper. Piero said he needed to go into the city, too, and would give me a ride.

I quickly showered, threw on a cotton skirt and sweater, and rushed back to the courtyard, like a schoolgirl fretting she would be late for class. "*Stai calma*," Piero said. Relax. "Why are Americans always in such a hurry?" I chuckled and told him Lawrence's comment: "If you want a slow tempo — *adagio, adagio* — you can slow down to such a pitch that you're faintly moving backwards here in Italy."

Piero laughed just as he spoke: from the core of his being. Unfortunately, he drove with similar gusto. On the trip into Florence, I clutched my armrest and held my breath at every jagged turn. Meanwhile, he talked animatedly — about literature and life, Shakespeare and obscure English poets, and the beauty of Florence at night.

When we arrived in town, he asked if I would join him for an *aperitivo* before I left for dinner. We sat at the bar and drank *Negronis* — potent concoctions of gin, sweet vermouth and *Campari*. As we talked and he smoked, he told me the one thing he loved about America was Walt Whitman. I could hardly believe it; I had cherished Whitman since college.

I told Piero about my love of Whitman. I explained how Lawrence thought Whitman was the greatest American writer and how the poet sparked Lawrence's interest in America. Piero confessed that he had never liked Lawrence's work, and I agreed not to hold this against him. Our *aperitivo* turned into dinner. Dinner evolved into exploring the streets of Florence late into the night: strolling into the *Piazza della Repubblica*, street dancing in the ancient square, sharing a nightcap at a pub beside the *Duomo*.

As we drove back to the Podoro estate, I looked at Piero. He was not at all a handsome man, but one of the most attractive I'd ever met.

The next morning I woke up late and walked out into the villa's courtyard just before noon.

"*Buon giorno, Principessa!*" Piero said, as he crossed the farm's field.

"Is it still technically *giorno?*" I teased. "I can't believe it's so late."

"It's good for you," he said, grinning. "Remember — *adagio, adagio.*"

He grabbed my hand. "Come on," he said, "I want to show you around." We ambled through the *vendemmia*. San Giovese, Chardonnay, white and red Trebbiano grapes hung, supple, from the vines. The rest of the grounds boasted terraced arbors covered with kiwi fruit, walnut and chestnut trees, pomegranates, persimmons, citrus, apples, pears, peaches, wisteria vines, tomatoes, potatoes, basil, sage, rosemary, verbena, lavender. The symphony of scents seduced me. Piero picked a fig for me to eat from a tree. When I bit into the sweet fruit, juice rolled down my chin.

In the olive groves, Piero explained how to "comb" the branches. He whistled as we walked through his land. I realized, for as long as I could remember, I had dreamed of stomping grapes in Italy and picking olives for the fall harvest. Now I was here amidst both olives and grapes with a man who cultivated my passions.

The next few days were a celebration of the senses, like Italy herself. Piero and I cooked lunch in the villa's large, ancient kitchen. We tasted as we prepared a variation of a *puttanesca* sauce — tuna, capers, tomatoes, parsley, garlic and rich, verdant olive oil, that would cover our hand-cut spaghetti. We wandered through the dusty, gilded church of San Miniato, where the remains of famous Florentines resided. I watched birds outside Piero's cottage, which was nestled in a secluded corner of the vineyard. We read: in silence, and then aloud for our favorite passages from Shakespeare, Whitman, Lawrence and Gibran. He played with my hand under the table at languorous dinners with foreign guests. I marveled as he glided effortlessly between French, Italian, German and Portugese. We tasted grapes as we sauntered through the *vendemmia* on his daily inspections.

I did not want these Tuscan days to end. My senses were filled. My rhythm had slowed. But I also began to feel guilty that during these days with Piero I had not advanced my research enough. Then I realized, I was no longer just studying Lawrence's life, I was *living it*. If only for a brief time, I had taken the author's life as my own and, in the process, I was transformed.

Sowing La Dolce Vita

Gloria, an Italian American, told me, "Probably the biggest eye-opener, and thrill, for me was the ten years of going back and forth to Iran, for about a month at a time. And to really know, understand, and feel comfortable with people of an entirely different culture that was initially so mysterious and foreign.

"One of the things that endeared them so much to me was

how they opened up their hearts to me," she continued. "Not just because a member of our family was married to one of theirs. It was because we were Italian. I was able to address that with a woman who lived in Tehran. I asked why they seemed to really love the Italian people.

" 'Because they are of our heart,' she said. 'They think like we do. They have a great love of life and their spirit is one of great happiness and positive attitudes. And their hospitality is very similar to ours, in terms of the food,' " Gloria recounted.

"They also wanted to know how I felt about them. And I had just been to Italy, and I said, 'You know, the minute I came into Iran, I didn't feel as much at home with my own people, so to speak, as I did with the Persians.' I got to know their language. I got to know their food. And the people themselves and the good hearts that they have; they are extremely refined, kind, very sensitive and intelligent. And my biggest answer to them was to say that 'I felt like I had packed my bags and come home.' "

How had Gloria experienced such an intimate view of their culture? "My favorite niece married a Persian man and they went to live in Iran," she said. "And, every year, my sister and I would travel somewhere together. At the time, my parents still had a home in southern Italy, so we would go there first, then we'd end up in Iran to visit her."

And the most memorable aspect of Gloria's time there was "The opening up of their homes to us," she said. "The home is extremely important. There was very little dining in restaurants, although we would do that now and again. The main thing was to have you in their home, and to greet you with great love and affection. And to present their very best to you; and their food is the best food I have had anywhere in the world. I did not know that. I knew very little about Persian food and customs. But the food and the process of serving it, and eating it together, and being joyous over everything that is theirs is yours..." she said.

"The dinner is such an exciting part of their life, their gusto. They would have these massive dinners that lasted the whole evening, with tables and tables full of food. Like one whole table when you'd arrive was just beautiful fruits, and then, some of my favorites they had were *khoresh bademjan,* which is braised lamb with eggplant, and it's this wonderful presentation with rice. And then another dish is *fesenjan.* And this is chicken or duck they soak and serve with walnuts and pomegranate juice. It's very sweet and spicy. And they have a way that they make rice like I've never seen. It's called *tahdic.* After they cook their rice — long grain Persian rice — they kind of stew it for a while, steam it. Then they take a ton of oil and butter and put it on the bottom of the pan, almost like it's burnt. And it is absolutely the most delicious thing I've ever tasted," Gloria said. "Naturally I have to go to the food first, because I'm Italian," she laughed.

"They have these beautiful presentations, far more elaborate than Italians. And it was very pervasive. It wasn't just the aristocracy. It was many people."

Reflecting on her experiences in this culture that first seemed so "mysterious and foreign," she said, "I think one of the great gifts of travel is that, because it's experiencing the unknown, you really must have an open mind and be willing to take whatever comes at that moment and enjoy that precious moment. I felt that way particularly in Iran."

But I learned that Gloria also transports that spirit home. "That sense of wonderment — which is what travel does to you, wondering what is around the next corner — we can bring that home, if we have that wanderlust in our hearts.

"Even if I'm just going to the store to go shopping," she said, "I always try to take a route I don't know. I try to experience a different way of coming home because I'll never learn anything if I always take the same way home. So I experience a different street, a different little community, sidewalks and trees. I see different houses and gardens and flowers. I liken it to traveling because you never know what's going to be around the next corner," she said.

On the afternoon that I interviewed Gloria, she had just come from a hospital visit to see a friend, who was one of several critically ill companions that Gloria regularly cared for. "I did that today, going to the hospital," Gloria said. "I took a completely different route and got totally lost. And I was laughing so hard at myself I had to stop on the side of the road to laugh. It was my own little way of traveling to someplace new," she said, "and only traveling in my head."

Perhaps this was what helped make Gloria a comforting caregiver. She kept finding ways to fuel her own joy so, when she arrived with others, she had plenty to share.

◈

Slow Down and Live in the Moment

1. *Slow down with a "Sensuality Day"* and surround yourself with elements you love: favorite foods, wines, books, music, clothes, friends, or stories to share.

2. *Be a writer for a day.* Savor all of your senses one at a time. Delight in creating comparisons, wordsmithing, to discover new ways to experience your sensory journey

3. *Develop your own "In-the-Moment" practice.* Will you meditate like Mark? Follow new routes when you run errands like Gloria? Walk every morning? Or practice yoga, make pottery, sketch or journal to slow down and live in the moment daily?

Chapter 5

Connect with the Power of Nature and Find Your Wild Side

RACING NIGHTFALL IN THE FADING LIGHT of Kenya's Masai Mara, we hurtled toward our campsite in two Land Rovers. Suddenly, our guide Makau, in the lead vehicle, turned and blazed in the opposite direction. He radioed our truck to follow him. He thought he had spotted something in the distance.

Within five minutes, we had reached a lion and lioness dozing in the plains. We pulled our vehicles within twelve feet of the animals and cut our motors. The cats rested on their sides, facing each other. The lion's long, golden mane, flecked with black and auburn, draped over the tips of the brown, grassy terrain.

Big cats rest up to twenty hours a day, so watching them sleep is routine. But after several minutes, the lion raised his head and bellowed a thunderous roar. The boom pounded through my chest and reverberated through my arms.

Had we agitated the lion? If so, what now? We were the only humans in sight.

The lioness raised to her two front paws.

The lion mounted her, roughly.

She sank back to the ground. Her head slung low, hovering just above the earth. Her front paws faced forward, neatly beneath her chin. She fixed her gaze on us. Her golden eyes rimmed perfectly with black, as if they had been stenciled on.

For a moment, I felt awkward, as if we were somehow intruding. But I quickly realized we were witnessing a magnificent, raw act: nature at its most base, and its most sublime.

I thought of what Denys Finch Hatton said in the movie, *Out of Africa*. He said that he liked animals so much because they "don't do anything half-heartedly. Everything is for the first time."

I, too, greatly prized this trait.

The lion sunk his teeth into the furry pocket behind the lioness's ear: a love bite.

The lioness roared and turned her face toward his. The lion's pale-brown spotted forehead creased. He lowered his haunches. His back arched. He growled, and bared his yellowing teeth. For an instant he transformed from the august master of this kingdom to a crouched, preying hyena: primal, rabid, ravishing. Within moments, both animals were asleep.

In the forty-five minutes that we stood there, our heads poked through the open roofs of the Land Rovers, the pair mated three times. Each time, the lioness's docile gaze remained fixed on us.

I felt a strange elation — akin to invincibility — after witnessing this act: staring into the lioness's eyes. Karen Blixen once expressed how I felt. "Lions possess a greatness, a majesty," she said. "Suddenly [one] comes to feel the mighty power of nature, when one looks it right in the eyes."

Embracing the Power of Nature ✐

Barbi, a designer, artist and teacher, experienced "a different kind of power, a really raw power of Mother Nature," when she encountered a flash flood on a backpacking trip in the Grand Canyon.

"I went hiking in the Grand Canyon for the first time in high school, as part of an earth science class, and my brother happened to be in that same class," she said. "Subsequently, my brother started hiking there, and I've gone backpacking there numerous times since, on un-maintained, permitted, backcountry trails. They allow six permits at a time, and we go for one week at a time."

Barbi said she'd always enjoyed the self-sufficiency inherent in the experience. "You are carrying everything on your back, everything you need. And you are self-contained. I still love that today. That everything you need is on your back.

"You string up your backpack at night so animals can't get at it," she said. As Barbi spoke, I thought of how carrying all you need on your back in nature and protecting it is a good equalizer, a connector. Suddenly, you need to think as an animal. Knowing that you, too, are now part of the food chain: vulnerable, as they are.

"That particular day of the flash flood, I happened to journal while the sun was going down and we were getting ready for dinner," Barbi said. "I made some comments in my journal that everyone in our group seemed a bit anxious. And all the little frogs that were typically around were moving uphill. And all the creatures that seemed to be around — the gnats and flies — were noticeably gone, as if they knew something that we didn't. There was a stillness that was coming.

"We could see spotty clouds up on the rim and could tell there was some rain happening, but there was nothing over us, or near us. It was about ten o'clock, and we had just laid down, three in a tent, when my brother yelled, 'Get out! Get out!' He knew exactly what it was, even though he had never experienced it before.

"I had no idea what I was running from. I ran barefoot. I had boxer shorts on. I didn't have any top on because I was getting ready for sleep. And I fell flat on my chest, on a bed of rocks, and I could feel it in my chest. Then I turned my head up and there was this tongue of water; a very narrow tongue that was out ahead of this wall of water. And they were yelling at me, 'Get up! Get up!' They were already up on higher ground, and I was lying there thinking, *What's going on?*

"Our camp was split by the water. Two people ended up on a ledge as their tent went down river with the light on. We didn't know if they were alive or dead. I broke my ankle running through the water, so I was in shock. We lost our gear, our boots; we lost everything.

"The next morning, when daylight came, two people volunteered to leave, because we were really remote in the canyon. They had to get out, with almost no water, and get help.

"They hiked out, and ten hours later were at the Forest Service. When the Forest Service came down, they said the water was six-feet high and ninety-feet wide. The helicopter ended up taking all of us out of there, and they declared it a natural disaster."

The experience taught Barbi much. "You can't underestimate the power of Mother Nature. When you go to wild places like that, you need to know what you are doing — and be conscious," she said. "That was a huge lesson for me regarding my own intuition. I was very aware that something was different in the environment. The little creatures were already telling us that something was happening. And there was a silence that doesn't typically exist. Even the angst between all of us was very present," she said.

"I think being in nature touches the core of my being," Barbi reflected. "It makes me remember, on a very intimate level, that I am not different than that frog going up that hill, or that plant life. I really see the interconnectedness of everything. And I am aware of all of those pieces that make up the whole of who I am, and who you are, and the bigness of this world. I think, in our day-to-day life, we just lose track of that. *I* lose track of that," she said. "I think being in nature in these ways allows me to really embrace my own power."

Barbi and I spoke for more than an hour about her canyon experiences. And toward the end, she said, "What comes to me when I'm in the canyon, and what I try to bring home, is that will to live. Not just to survive — but to *live, fully*. I think it's so important to be able to stay in touch with that. And it takes work. That will to live: to live your *fullness*. We can get so disconnected with that. I think we get inhibited because we become afraid of what people are going to think. Or all those signs that say, 'Stop.' So we get quieted."

Barbi now had tears in her eyes. I watched her, as she paused, grew silent. It was as if she were recalling the power she had experienced, *known* in the canyon, and was determined to summon once more in her daily life: like the bull who paws the ground before his final surge with new power.

"At this point of my life, I'm not quiet anymore," Barbi declared. "I can't be silent anymore. We have to live out loud, and be who we are. And if somebody doesn't like us as we are, too bad. The people that are there with you are really with you. It's like the message that the Hopi leader gave at the beginning of the new millennium. He talks about don't hang on to the shore. Go to the middle of the river; and look around, and see who's there with you. Don't cling to the shore because that's basically an illusion. Allow the river to carry you."

And Barbi has returned to backpack in the canyon many times since the day of the flood, always striving — at home and on the road — to let the river carry her.

Living Out Loud

"A man who lives fully is prepared to die at any time," Ed Abbey said. Abbey's hunger for life seduced me. He courted gluttony, for "women, books, adventure, travel, music, philosophy, color and form." His diaries revealed that he had a "brilliant appetite for life, for every moment, every detail." And, according to his friend and biographer, Jack Loeffler, Abbey's "soul was on fire."

Some people described Abbey as raw, coarse, brutish. These qualities did not bother me. They helped complete a picture of a complex man.

Born in Appalachia, "Cactus Ed" discovered the Southwest as a teenager and pined for it until he could live there permanently. After moving west, Abbey would become one of the most influential nature writers of the twentieth century. He wrote sixteen books during his life, including pivotal works such as *Desert Solitaire* and *The Monkey Wrench Gang*. Five additional books were published posthumously. And his provocative writings would prove prophetic to an ever-expanding audience after his death.

Abbey also worked as a ranger in sixteen national parks and forests, and in several nature preserves. His service in Aravaipa Canyon was his longest stint anywhere. He worked on and off in the canyon for two years in the early 1970s, and Aravaipa gave Abbey much. It became the setting for a chapter in *The Fool's Progress*. He wrote much of *The Monkey Wrench Gang* there. It inspired essays such as "Freedom and Wilderness," "Aravaipa Canyon," and "Merry Christmas, Pigs!" and played host to some of his most poignant wildlife encounters. Biographers have said this was one of the happiest times in Abbey's life, and he agreed. "I should be as happy as a pig in shit," he said. "And I am."

Abbey rallied to preserve the environment. Wilderness, he claimed, was a place of psychic refuge: something humans need desperately. He urged people to get out into nature as much as possible, not in cars, but to walk, "better yet, crawl," as he declared in *Desert Solitaire*.

As I set out into Aravaipa Canyon, I would heed Abbey's call; this time backpacking with a companion who shared my desire to learn more about the fiery author and the wilds of Arizona.

Glimpsing a Wild Side ✍

Richard and I had settled into a comfortable camaraderie, as we sloshed through Aravaipa Creek in silence. A trail meandered in and out of the stream for nearly twelve miles through this rugged, remote gorge in southeastern Arizona. The preserve also boasted myriad wildlife, including mountain lion, desert bighorn sheep, ringtail cat, javelina, and over two hundred species of birds. I wanted to find the wild side.

Serenity blanketed the canyon. Water glistened like crystal in places, and minnows swam past us, to wherever it was they were headed. Butterflies with names like Queen, Mourning Cloak, and Empress Leilia fluttered against a cerulean sky. A Steller Jay flew from a bough in the creek, leading us upstream.

Suddenly, we spotted a most incongruous combination: a Great Blue Heron perched on the water, and a large javelina by its side, snout immersed in creek vegetation. The moment we paused, the heron took off, flying over us, its long elegant wings outstretched. The stout, pig-like animal continued eating: his short, slender legs sunk in the sand and his grizzled gray hair moving faintly as he foraged.

We rounded the bend and noticed the javelina was not alone. Another peccary, slightly smaller, stood behind him with two young ones. His family. When we drew closer, the mother and children continued grazing along the banks: unaware, or unconcerned, by our presence. But the patriarch grew curious instantly.

He walked to the land, through the brush, toward us. Not fast, but slowly and deliberately.

"What do you think we should do?" Richard whispered.

"I'm not sure. I remember Abbey wrote about wandering into a pack of javelina here one Christmas night," I said, racking my brain about how the story ended. I also recalled that peccary could be merciless to dogs and dangerous to aggressive humans, especially when their young were near. "I think it's okay if we just walk gently," I replied.

"Alright," Richard said, already striding. He'd kidded earlier that he was not interested in any intimate encounters with mammals bearing sharp tusks or large teeth: Javelina, for example.

The mother and children scampered across the water to the opposite bank. I inched closer to the lone javelina. He had stopped about ten feet from where Richard and I had stood. His wiry hair now looked like porcupine quills. His massive round head would have reached just above my knees if I were standing by his side. I hoped he would stay, his pronged hooves planted in the wet dirt. But he resumed walking into the brush.

Tangled branches revealed two bushy ears, backlit and translucent, poking from beneath a bough. Gingerly, I stepped up the muddy slope. He moved another pace toward me. Now we were eye to eye. Brushwood cropped his snout, tusks, and the top of his head. So I saw only eyes. And he saw mine. His soft brown eyes glistened in the sunlight. They looked beautiful, and, somehow, utterly innocent.

What was this urge to get close to animals in the wild? To cross a boundary. Feel an immediacy. Experience the charge of connection.

I wanted to tear off my backpack, shed my clothes and run

through the stream — my feet, like hooves, secure on the rocky creek floor. I wanted to charge through the brush, scamper up jagged inclines, sure and steadfast. I wanted to forage and find shelter with this family under falling stars.

The javelina and I stared at each other for another minute, maybe more. Then he stepped backward, breaking the spell. When I started upstream, he disappeared into the brush, as suddenly as he had appeared.

When I joined Richard, I grabbed his hand. "That was amazing," I said. I wanted to share this with him but somehow words didn't suffice. I tried to describe the light, the moment, my feeling. The rest, I guess, would remain between the javelina and me.

But as we wandered upstream, I remembered Ed Abbey's words which, today, I felt could be my own: "I felt what I always feel when I meet a large animal face to face in the wild. I felt a kind of affection and the crazy desire to communicate, to make some kind of emotional, even physical, contact with the animal."

Richard and I looked back as we rounded a curve and glimpsed the male javelina trotting across the creek, to join his family. Richard squeezed my hand and we meandered on, together, in silence.

Finding Distant Relatives

Glenn, an insurance executive, who'd "seen animals in zoos" but had never felt a fervent interest in wildlife, said, "When *Gorillas in the Mist* came out as a book and then as a movie, I read and saw it and said to my wife, 'I am going there.'

"So I booked a flight through Nairobi and, without reservations, went on my own.

"I was greeted at the airport by a young Rwandan with a new Jeep I had rented. She then pointed me in the direction of the Virunga Volcanoes and off I went.

"Two hours later, with the help of basic French, I found the tiny town of Ruhengera and checked into a small stuccoed motel.

"The next morning I got up early and drove eighteen kilometers to the starting point for the trek into the jungle and joined seven others. They allow eight people per visit with the gorillas. And you're allowed one hour with them, not a minute longer. They don't want the gorillas to become over-habituated.

"We then hiked and hacked through the jungle with machetes and two guards carrying ancient rifles. After about four and a half hours of slogging around in miserable rain, we came upon a family with the head honcho silverback. It was overcast and not a great experience. Very difficult to see and take pictures," Glenn said.

"We returned, slipping and sliding, convinced we would not return the next day. But the next morning at seven, I heard a knock on my door and one of the women in the group said, 'Let's go.' So on went the muddy boots and clothes of the previous day and off we went.

"In a forty-five-minute, light hike through the jungle with beautiful sunshine, we came across a perfect family of gorillas. There were ten to fifteen of them, counting the little ones. And I had the young gorillas brushing against me, all showing off. Just like kids in a park. Tumbling and tagging and constantly looking to make sure you're watching them.

"The guards ask you not to come within twenty feet of the gorillas. But sometimes it's impossible to avoid contact when the little ones are playing tag and scampering at your feet.

"In the perimeter was the silverback, who is the head of the family. And that, of course, was the one we were told to look out for and avoid eye contact, and to drop to the ground if he started approaching. And to grunt, which is their language.

"Then I was taking a picture of a mother gorilla with a three-week old infant breast-feeding. And suddenly she charged. The guide and I were standing shoulder-to-shoulder. I just ducked out of the way and she hit him instead. And he went flying, knocked him flat. And she went back to nursing as if to say, 'I need privacy. Leave me alone.' "

So, how did Glenn feel amidst these "gentle giants," as they sometimes have been called?

"It was like looking at a distant relative," Glenn said.

In fact, it was such a "fantastic, memorable experience that made the entire trip worthwhile," that Glenn "struck up a dialogue with the U.S. Embassy the next day, and they put me in touch with the Rwandan Ambassador stationed in D.C."

This move would change Glenn's life.

"The ambassador invited me to visit with him. He then came to Chicago to see the Midwest. I flew him all around in my plane, and then he invited me to represent the Republic of Rwanda as Honorary Consul, which I accepted. Sometime later I was promoted to Honorary Consul General.

"The experience has been fantastic," Glenn said. "I have returned to Rwanda several times and I now also serve on the Board of the Dian Fossey International Gorilla Fund to help conserve the gorillas. And when they're gone, they're gone," he said. "There aren't any more mountain gorillas in the world."

Connect with the Power of Nature and Find Your Wild Side

1. *Allow nature to become a theme in your travels.*
   Track gorillas in Africa. Hike in the Grand Canyon.
   Swim with dolphins in the Bahamas. And in all future
   trips, seek to spend an hour in nature and watch the
   light change.

2. *Cultivate the connection back home.* Select a spot
   in nature and visit there for a half-hour every week.
   Enjoy as your observations of the place, and yourself
   in it, grow.

3. *"Adopt" a wild animal.* Study an animal that has
   always interested you. Ask yourself what you can
   learn from that animal, what qualities does it possess
   that you might desire more of in your life?

Chapter 6

Feel Sexy

WHILE WRITING THIS CHAPTER, I met a woman in a café, a new bride who had just turned thirty-five. She had lived and modeled in Paris in her twenties and told me, "I did some of the biggest runway shows in Paris, with designers like Jean Paul Gauthier and Galiano." Later she moved to New York, where she continued to surround herself with beautiful friends and acquaintances. Yet when I asked what she thought was key to being sexy, she said, "Sexy is something that comes from within. I have seen some of the most fabulously gorgeous women with no sex appeal. I don't know whether they haven't quite figured out their bodies yet, or they just don't have it inside them. Sexy is something that comes from the soul," she said. "And you just exude it."

The Hemingway Touch

I was not attracted to my initial impression of Hemingway. Of course I liked that he was an adventurer and traveler. Otherwise, however, I imagined him largely brash, boorish, bullish in his male bravado. Yet I wondered if he hid behind this larger-than-life façade. I began to read biographies about him. I started to see his vulnerabilities, his complexities. I learned that he was easy to cry, very sensitive, and that he was incredibly loyal to friends. I started to feel drawn to him.

There was something "magnetic" about Hemingway, as his friends would often say. They also said that he "did everything to the hilt," had a "radiance and presence" that some likened to John F. Kennedy. He "was the kind of man to whom men, women, children and dogs were attracted" and that Hemingway was "the most exuberant, active, enthusiastic man anyone met."

How could I not love a man of passion, insatiable curiosity, and radiance? One who had the ability to bring a *joie de vivre* to everything he did.

"Papa" found an adopted homeland in Cuba. He explored and wrote about many international locales — including France, Spain, Italy, and Africa. Only of Cuba, though, did Hemingway say that he wanted to stay forever.

He also penned some of his best works there. Hemingway completed *For Whom the Bell Tolls* at "Finca Vigia," his home for many years. He also wrote *Across the River and into the Trees, The Old Man and the Sea,* and *A Moveable Feast* while there. *Islands in the Stream* — arguably his most autobiographical work — was published posthumously. Three of Hemingway's eight novels were set in Cuba — more than in any other country.

Hemingway called himself "*Cubano sato,*" a Cuban dialect phrase meaning flirt and half-breed. For Hemingway, flirting offered another means to engagement with life: inviting interaction from others, exploring connections.

Deep-sea fishing was Hemingway's dominant passion while he lived in Havana. Samuel Feijoo, a Cuban writer and artist, recounted going fishing with Hemingway one day. He said, "When we docked, everybody came to greet [Hemingway]: prostitutes, pimps, smugglers." And Hemingway told Feijoo, "I need affection. I don't care where it comes from." Papa also later told Feijoo, "I'm looking for solidarity. That's why I came to Cuba."

Hemingway did find the solidarity he was seeking in Cuba. His compassion for the Cubans moved him to rededicate his 1954 Nobel Prize for *The Old Man and the Sea* to those who had inspired his story. He lived on the island for more than twenty years and, as Gabriel Garcia Marquez said in *Hemingway in Cuba*, Papa met people of the sea "who were to become his friends until he died."

Until I traveled in Hemingway's path, I didn't know that I, too, sought some solidarity, a bond that I felt missing in my life. Ultimately, I would find a means of connection that I could carry with me forever.

Sexy as a Soul Story

A group of mostly American women, ranging from their early twenties to early sixties, gathered together, on an old Havana theater stage. We would take dance lessons here for the next two weeks. Two lithe, animated Cuban instructors led the class, and often would invite one of the twenty-something women to demonstrate with them. The young women would laugh and smile as they were swirled and spun.

I didn't mind the teachers' focus on these women. In fact, I thought, if I were them, I would be attracted to that vitality too. But it felt odd. For much of my life I had felt real exuberance. Now, hurtling toward forty, I felt some of it drain, wane. Though I had danced salsa for years, I felt awkward and clumsy, tired and worn. I wondered if this was part of what older women friends had described. "After fifty," some would say, "you become invisible to men." But I couldn't quite believe that. These friends clearly had not lost their desire to be admired, but had lost an expectation that they would be.

What happened to us?

I tucked these thoughts away, into the back of my mind, as I headed out onto Hemingway's path.

I slept at the Ambos Mundos hotel, in the floor below Hemingway's Room 511, where he had his affair with Mrs. M., the woman who inspired the character Helene Bradley in *To Have and Have Not*. I drank "Papa Hemingway" daiquiris at Hemingway's favorite bar, the Floridita, and gazed at photos of him that lined the walls. I sipped *mojitos* at another of his chosen watering holes, the Bodeguita, and visited "Finca Vigia," his home outside Havana. I ate one of his favorite dishes, crab cooked in lemon and butter, in Cojimar, where Hemingway docked his boat for years.

I followed in Hemingway's trail for several days. Then I decided it was time to step away from his path, see where *my* dominant passion – dance – might lead me.

Music and dance were everywhere. Songs swelled from bands in the street, emanated from cassette players in houses with open windows and doors. A street barber cut hair to sounds from a tattered tape recorder he had placed beside him. Kids in a cobbled lane played clave rhythms on an empty rum bottle with a stone. Music flowed from courtyards, patios and back alleys. Couples danced on the street, in doorways and in coffee bars. School-children moved to music that spilled from neighborhood cafés.

Just as music and dance seemed part of the Cuban soul, so did sensuality. Men and women freely checked each other out as they passed on the street. The exchange did not feel predatory or threatening, but, rather, revealed an open appreciation of other peoples' bodies and their movement. When couples walked together, men fastened their hands around women's waists, or buttocks or shoulders. Or held hands with their partner. Women swayed their bodies with abandon as they strode, whether alone or with a man. Surplus flesh was not a sin. Their beauty swelled from within. I realized, Cuban sensuality was a state of mind, and it was infectious.

I attended "Rumba Saturday," which felt like a large block party. People were laughing, chatting, greeting friends. Many of the Cuban men shook hands and hugged simultaneously.

I wanted to see the Cuban dance. Historically, rumba had been danced mostly in urban streets and barrios. Now it had become one of the country's most fashionable dances. Similar to the rumba that was so popular in America during the 1930s, the Cuban version was much more erotic — eroticism and enticement were bedrocks of the dance.

The object of rumba is male pursuit of a female partner, and her fanciful flight. The man employs various parts of his body to lure her: a hand, foot, elbow or his pelvis. The *vacunao*, or pelvic thrust, emanates from the Spanish term "to vaccinate," and symbolizes penetration. The woman seductively evades these advances. Throughout, the partners strive to show the sensuality of the woman and the allure of the man.

I watched as the crowd quieted when, in the center of the stage, a woman in her late forties or early fifties started to dance with a man in his twenties. He was barefoot, with sleepy eyes and a trimmed goatee, and wore a form-fitting, white sleeveless T-shirt and beige pants with the cuffs rolled up. The woman was not at all classically beautiful. She was plump and had thick, unruly hair and a wide gap between her front teeth. But she began her dance with utter confidence, grace, and style. She waved the side of her skirt like a matador, and flirted with her eyes, as if challenging her partner to attempt a *vacunao*.

The man expressed a range of facial expressions as he danced, from pained to predatory. She shimmied and spun away from him as he approached. She rippled her body, vibrating the musical accent, extending the pulse. The man crouched low, thrust his pelvis toward her unexpectedly. She swiped a pink washcloth over her pelvic region, then grinned and turned, still glancing at the man over her shoulder.

The man and woman continued to weave this tapestry of invitation and elusion, pursuit and evasion: spinning a universal story with their dance.

Later that evening, I had my own chance to dance.

A booming, restless beat coursed through the Casa de Musica as I entered. Men wore collared shirts, hockey jerseys, and newsboy caps. Women sported spandex pants, cropped halter-tops, and tight floral dresses. Several men patted their chests to the music, drumming their hearts. An air of celebration permeated the dark, smoky club.

I noticed one of my dance school's drumming teachers, Daniel, standing with a group from the academy. He looked dapper dressed all in white: a crisp newsboy's cap, hockey jersey, pleated pants, loosely laced sneakers, and two gold chains draped around his neck.

I said hello and walked to the bar. When I returned, a woman standing by his table swayed alone to the music as she sipped from a glass of rum. Her melon-shaped bottom swung in perfect synchronization to the sounds.

I tried to mimic her moves, subtly: the soft rhythm of her hips; the small, circuitous circles she created to the clave beat; the delicate ripples that started in the small of her back and flowed upward, undulating through her torso like swells in the sea.

Daniel came up behind me and placed his hands on my hips. He began to move me so I mirrored the woman's motion. He had seen me trying to mimic her. He guided my hips to the left… back…forward…right. Each time creating a long, even, figure eight, so smooth the movement felt liquid.

When I attempted the motion on my own, my hips rolled freely, but created a circle, rather than a figure eight. *"Está como sexo,"* Daniel whispered in my ear. *It's like sex.* His comment surprised me, but felt neither disrespectful nor suggestive; rather, perfectly natural.

I settled into the motion and Daniel continued to lead me. *"Abajo,"* he said softly. I bent my knees and sank lower. *"Sube,"* he said, and I slithered up, tracing loose figure eights with my hips as I rose.

He took my hand and led me to the dance floor. He spun me. Crouched low to turn me by rotating my calf. Dipped me. I straddled his thigh as I arched back, my right arm limp like a rag doll. He swept me from right to left in a long, gentle arc. Then shimmied down my body. And released me.

I shook my shoulders, swiveled my hips, pulsed my chest, belly, hips and thighs. Dancing apart but still with Daniel, the music seemed to surge through my body, course through my veins. I realized, suddenly, that something about me is only wholly articulated in dance: Only in dance does my true sensuality express itself.

I walked through the streets of Havana the next two days feeling exuberant. I felt the sway of the Cuban women, and an awareness of my body I had never experienced before. I wanted to remember this feeling always, and live the full *me* that had shown up on the dance floor.

When I returned from Cuba, I felt more vibrant and alive than ever. I threw myself into dancing, several nights a week: immersing myself in the sounds and sways of rumba, salsa, and tango. I even learned a new dance, West Coast Swing, and joined an amateur performance team.

But I forgot to transport this newfound sensuality from the dance floor into my everyday life. To recall it, I would need to gather the pieces that had become fragmented in some way. Wisdom from fellow female travelers would help guide me.

Discovering You "Have It"

Roz, a grandmother of two, in her seventies, told me:

"I was a young career girl with a few years behind me, but I was still living at home. I went to my paymaster and said, 'I want you to take $25 from my paycheck every week for what I called my 'Travel Adventure Fund.'

"It was 1948 and I made a point that, when I hit $1,000 or $1,200, I would go to Europe. Then a colleague from work asked if I wanted to go on a cruise.

"And this was the era of Wallis Simpson and The Duke of Windsor, and you dressed for dinner to the nines every night. Everything was very formal, you know: bouillon at eleven, tea in the afternoon.

"The cruise was from New York to Havana, then on to other ports. And I wore these gorgeous, very daring evening dresses: backless. Can you imagine that? An evening dress without a back?

"I came from a family of musicians and studied piano from the age of five, so I had music in my soul. And what do you have in Havana but the rumba? That marvelous, sexy Latin beat... And those were the years of complete decadence. This was before Fidel; this was Batista. And there was a rum-running scheme, and there was prostitution. It was very wild and licentious. And that was its lore and allure — along with the music.

"A Cuban writer, who had come to interview passengers on the boat, took me into Havana on my first night. And what do you see and hear? You hear rumba bands, and the music, and the gambling, and the high-class prostitution, and it was all very exciting," she said.

"So here I was in this utterly sexy, forbidden, romantic atmosphere of this constant rumba, and I love the Latin music, I adore it to this day. And that atmosphere of dancing and rhythm and sex: *seduction* is the word.

"And the first officer of my cruise ship fell in love with me. It was a love that was more than love. It was sexual obsession. *He had to have me.* I didn't have that much experience, so it was a big thing for me to handle. And this went on for about a year and a half after the cruise was over and I came back to New York. He sent me love letters and wires and mail from all over the world," she said.

"So that is something that has changed my life. I think I discovered my basic sexuality on that trip," Roz said.

"The next trip was the most transforming experience in my life," she said. "It was 1952 and I had about $1,200 from the payroll girl. So I went to Europe, alone. And it changed my life. *Changed my life.*

"I still had some looks then, and I was just bursting to see and to love and to experience. I didn't even want to sleep. I couldn't wait for the next day. I would get up and say, 'What marvelous adventure am I going to have today? What marvelous thing is going to happen to me and make my heart soar with joy?' And something always did.

"And people respond to that kind of excitement," she said. "They *feel it.* You don't have to wear a placard, 'Hey look at me!' They just sense it. And I had such marvelous adventures. I also found a confidence that I never had before.

"My confidence came from the feeling that I was approachable and sexy to men," she added. "I think the excitement of doing the unknown had a lot to do with my attraction to them. And I think it was partly because I was open. And I just sort of knew that I 'had it.' That I was attractive, and that I was going to have some wonderful experiences.

"There were attractive men everywhere in Italy," she said,

"and I met lots of them.

"Do you remember that famous photograph by Ruth Orick?" Roz asked. As it turned out, I did. The photograph of an American woman walking down a street in Italy with men of various ages all watching, appreciating her, as she passed, hangs in my bedroom.

"That could've been *me!*" Roz said. "The Ruth Orick picture was 1951, and that was me in 1952."

One experience punctuated Roz's Italian sojourn that she still recalls today:

"My grandmother had a big, gorgeous house in Brooklyn before the Depression. And this beautiful mahogany bookcase that was always locked," Roz said. "I was about fourteen and a literary kid. I always loved reading. And there were all of these enticing books in there. So I watched that bookcase for years.

"One day, I was there and my grandmother was out in the sunroom with her Bible, and the bookcase was open. And I just went to that bookcase and, at random, picked out a book called *Europa*. Had never heard of the book, but just opened it. And I was enthralled. It was the story of aristocratic Europeans who were in love, and it was about their affairs, and life and travel. And they wanted to cram it all in before a war they knew was coming.

"One of the sequences was a woman who went to the Blue Grotto in Capri," Roz said. "She wanted to prove something to herself. She stood up in the boat and took off her bathing suit and swam, naked, in the Blue Grotto while the oarsman watched. How can you not remember that incident? And that was when I was fourteen years old.

"Then in 1952, I was in Capri. And I said, 'I am going to

do exactly what she did.' I went down to the Blue Grotto and I hired an oarsman and we paddled through. And we were the only ones, and the silence was spooky. All you could hear was the oar lapping in the water. And there I was, all alone, with these rocks that appeared to be lit by blue flames, and the water was so blue, it was overwhelming. And I stood up in the boat and I said to myself, 'Do I have the nerve? Will I do it? *Shall I do it?*'

"And I didn't have the courage," Roz said. "But I did hear someone say that, if you swim in the Blue Grotto, which you're not allowed to do, it brings you luck. And I jumped over and swam across the Blue Grotto, touching the rock walls for luck. I swam and I came back into the boat. The oarsman thought I was absolutely crazy and I said to him, '*Per fortuna!*' For good luck. And I ended it by knowing that I swam, and I dove, but a part of me was lost under the waters forever."

What had Roz meant, exactly, that a part of her was "lost under the waters forever"?

"What I meant was that the final thrust, the real adventure, the real me, the solo me, the persona that I wanted to be, like the woman in the book, if I had stripped and gone naked, it would have been a supreme statement. And *I didn't have the nerve.* I missed the nerve. I missed that feeling. I didn't have the guts to do it," she said.

While Roz might have felt she "missed the nerve," Barbi stepped in, fifty-odd years later.

Finding Full Female Power

"Being in the Grand Canyon, you feel like you want to rip off your clothes and run around naked," Barbi said. "And I've done it. And it feels great!

"When you're down there you feel so beautiful and radiant and you *are*. It's your essence coming out. And it's not about this shell that we walk around in that's so much of our culture," she said.

"My friend Susan and I really admire the river runner Katie Lee. She was a rebel in her time and we'd often talk about how she'd always hike in the buff when she was out in the canyon. She'd have her boots, and her hat, and she'd go everywhere. And Susan and I were saying we wanted our 'Katie Lee Photo.' I was just about to turn fifty; I was in my fiftieth year.

"Susan's husband's a photographer. I had never been naked in front of him, but I could not have cared less; nothing even had to be said. He just knew that when we went down there we wanted to be photographed in nature, in the nude. So it was not planned. And, all of the sudden, we were in Matkatamiba. A bunch of people were lying on the rocks, eating snacks, sketching and talking. And we said, 'This is the time.' So we hiked back down the narrows and got into these beautiful sculptural rocks, and we stripped down and were all over the rocks. It was very sensuous," she said.

"These beautiful sloped walls were smooth and they had the wear of age and history and they just warped to our bodies. So that their curves formed to our curves. And Rick was able to see that, not only in the geography but he saw it in us. So he would say, 'Go right there. Curve in that water.' And water was running over us. It was just so uninhibited; it was beautiful. It was like being in the womb of the earth. And, being a female experiencing that, it was so powerful," Barbi said.

Feeling Truly Beautiful for the First Time ✎

Melissa, a novelist in her fifties, wrote me after a sojourn in Italy:

"I was in Florence for the month of June. An entire month, a glorious month, all the trees and flowers in bloom, the air warm and scented — everywhere I walked, everywhere I looked I saw beauty or something deeply appealing to the senses — and isn't this the essence of sensuality — to appeal to the senses, to intoxicate and expand, open through the senses? So the atmosphere was seductive first of all.

"Then the Florentine people, who are both private and sociable, always with a cell phone to the ear, or simply taking great joy in conversations over lunch or while shopping or walking along... an animation, a vivaciousness tempered by privacy; a place where secrets can flourish in cool, dim shadows, just a few steps out of the warm, honeyed sunlight. A sense of extremes, the erotic and the stillness of sleep or death co-mingled, sex heightened by the preserved dead everywhere. A city made of stone and flesh, exquisite art, sculpture and a skeletoned mosaic of saints, heretics, merchants and whores, nuns and poets, musicians, mothers, cooks, politicians, bishops and jewelers.

"Food is prized, good, fresh food — eating is a daily, prime pleasure, as is the drinking of good wine. To linger over a table savoring food and wine, to stop for a coffee, a *gelato*, the open appreciation of the magical sustenance of food is everywhere.

"The Renaissance is the jeweled setting for the sexuality and sensuality of the present life in Florence.

"How could I not feel sensual, sexual, alive as eros means

completely alive, in this place? It is true, I walked differently, my body opening to itself, breasts not hidden by poor posture — unconsciously, unstudied, I swayed my hips, threw back my shoulders, proud in an instinctive, biologic way, of my femininity. I had no interest in having sex with anyone — I was ending one relationship back home and in the early fragile beginning stages of another. I did not choose the complication of an Italian lover. I prized my solitude, spent hours happily alone each day walking, conversing with strangers, flirting with waiters and shopkeepers — feeling somehow it was not only 'safe' but part of the culture — a celebration of the erotic dance — a mirror of nature, part of nature.

"I have never felt more beautiful or serene or joyful or comfortable, easy, with my female body. In America, I judged myself harshly and by magazines and by Hollywood standards of beauty — by such standards I failed, and so I had defaulted early on, in adolescence, from the notion or hope of ever being beautiful. It seemed too hard, too artificial, an exercise in copying, and failing to adequately copy, someone else. Here, in Florence, I felt uniquely beautiful, the same as any other woman passing by, of any age; she, too, was uniquely beautiful. Here was no generic standard to apply from the outside in. Here beauty emerged from the inside and any adornment simply magnified it. Here, beauty was a new freedom to be enjoyed and cherished.

"In America, I have never mastered the art of flirting, another game I defaulted from — feeling clumsy and unskilled. In Florence, when a man would pass by, of any age, and look at me with appreciation and frank sexuality in his eyes, saying '*Ciao, Bella,*' at first I was shocked and ducked my head, gradually I came to look him in the eyes as I passed, sometimes even smiling mysteriously — feeling thrilled, as though we had just fleetingly and in complete innocence, had a sexual meeting. The innocence and joy of this feeling completely amazed me — because it felt right, it felt like, *Ah, this is how men and women are supposed to acknowledge one another's attraction: by a glance, a greeting, then a moving on.* It is not personal; nothing complicated will happen; it is fun and profound at the same time. When I gave birth to my daughters, I felt I joined a long history of women. When I passed a man on the street in Florence who greeted me, when I looked back at him for those few seconds, as we gazed into each others' eyes for that charged moment, I felt I had entered the purest sexual territory of human beings, a territory that linked me to my race and its generative instincts.

"There was one day in particular, after a soccer match, when I happened to accidentally wander into back streets overflowing and rowdy with male soccer players and mostly male fans — at first I felt an old instinct to make myself invisible, 'small,' to succumb to feeling threatened by so much raw male energy. Then I realized, as I smiled at one good-looking young man who was frankly and appreciatively watching me pass by, that it was all right, it was safe — this was even to be enjoyed — and I walked the rest of the way through that maze of crowded streets, shoulders back, head high, feeling incredibly vibrant and beautiful. This was my beauty, no one else's, free of outside standards and judgments. I realized during that walk that here was the secret to true beauty, a beauty I could accept and reflect and believe in. True beauty was personal, it emanated from each woman, uniquely.

"I have never experienced thirty days of such complete,

unending bliss as I did in Florence that summer. Beauty, appetite, aesthetic joy, spirituality, all human desires and longings were fed richly each day, each hour. And when I came home, stepping off the plane dressed differently, having lost weight from so much walking — not from any diet! — wearing a black sleeveless sheath and a colored scarf around my hips, feeling, well, sexy, sensuous, slinky, and absolutely joyous, I knew for a certainty that my failing relationship was truly over when the man I had been living with took one look at me, wrinkled up his face in mild disgust and said, 'What are you wearing that for? It doesn't look good on you.' *What does he know?* I thought. *And what do I care? For the first time in my life I feel fully, gloriously, uncompetitively female and alive.*

"I have had some difficulty, back in America, retaining that sense of beauty, though now that I remember it and know what it feels like, I can remember to consciously pleasure my senses, slow down, walk openly, proudly. I can pay attention to my clothing, to what feels good and looks especially lovely to me. I can laugh, enjoy a dessert or a wine, a glance of pleasure, without guilt or anxiety. Being female, sensuous, sexy, is about openness — to life, to love, to participating in and celebrating in the exotic eros of each holy instant. In Florence, not only did I find my own beauty, but my secret belief that holiness and sexuality were aspects of the same divine bliss, was confirmed and evident everywhere, even in my dreams."

Remembering Who Creates It

While I finished my interview with Roz, she thanked me. "This trip down memory lane has given me a great lift," she said, "because I've been a bit down lately. I think aging has something to do with it," she added. "Like with the pain, you hurt. And when you hurt, it casts a pall over you. I was very blue a couple of months back, and I went to a dear friend and asked if she thought I was neurotic. I said that I find that I am looking back — I'm looking back on my youth and my romance and my love affairs and my travel, and the books say you should look *ahead* — live in the moment, plan now. And my friend said, 'Your memories are very entrenched in your persona. Remember, these things that you did and experienced; you made them happen.' And that reverberated in me," Roz said. "Yes, I made these things happen. I sought out adventure. I sought out the music. I did things on my own. And it paid me a great enrichment in my life that I wouldn't have otherwise had. And, as my friend also said, 'You are what you've lived. You've created this life. Take comfort in this.' "

Feel Sexy

1. *Flirt like an Italian, a Cuban or Hemingway.* No agenda, no objective: just the joy of engagement and interaction.

2. *Dance, dance, dance (or fish, fish, fish).* Throw yourself wholeheartedly into an interest. You might just uncover a passion within yourself you never knew you had.

3. *Be an actor for a day.* Study the local ways of flirting in a foreign land. Watch how people move their hands, hold their heads, smile, walk. Then practice their gestures. How do you feel in this new role?

Chapter 7

Step into Your Courage

"I STRIPPED DOWN TO MY BATHING SUIT and started to climb out over this area where tourists do not go," Michael, an entrepreneur, said. "I climbed out on this cliff and looked down into this blowhole, and it was deep! I couldn't believe that I was up on this precipice looking down at water surging up as little as fifty feet away — if you can call that little — and as much as one hundred and fifty feet away. And that water was moving at a good rate! It was welling up and then going back down. And I realized, if I didn't time my jump right, I could kill myself."

Michael was in Jamaica having a quiet beer at a bar "located in this oceanographic formation. Some people called the formation a blowhole, others called it 'the toilet bowl.' The cliffs in this area are one hundred and fifty to two hundred feet tall. And, over eons, as the water has hit the cliffs, it's eaten a hole in the bottom of the cliff. The top of the cliff has been eaten away at the center, probably a hundred feet across. So it's like a tube that goes all the way to the base of the cliffs. And the bar is situated on the edge of that; there is a cement sitting area that goes around the top of the hole.

"Jamaican cliff divers would go to the top of this sitting area and dive down into this formation, into this surging water, for money. The ocean tide would well up so it was within fifty feet of the top of the hole. Then, as the wave would recede, the water would go down as much as one hundred and fifty feet from the top of the hole. So the water was constantly going up and down inside this giant hole. And the cliff divers would dive after coins people had tossed in. Sometimes they would dive only fifty feet, which was a considerable distance anyway. Other times they would dive as much as one hundred and fifty feet because of the timing of the water surging up and down.

"Well, I happened to be a daredevil at the time and I like to take risks. And I was with my girlfriend who was saying, just for fun, 'You should do it. You'd be the only white boy here doing it.' Of course all the Jamaicans were doing it, but most of the people at the bar were Americans — probably two hundred people or so. And my girlfriend started egging me on. And I said, 'I can do it. I'm sure that I can do it.' Then other people heard us talking and started egging me on. And, before I knew it, the whole bar was saying, 'Go, go, go!' And I said, 'Okay, I'll do it.'

"So I asked the Jamaican guys how they did it, and they told me where to go. One guy went out to do it, and then showed me where the ladder was so I could climb all the way back up. And I said, 'I'm not going to dive, I'm just going to jump.'

"Then my knees started shaking," Michael said. "And I started to get concerned, because now I'd spent a good minute considering the possibilities. And I looked around and the crowd started saying, 'Jump! Jump! Jump! Jump!' And it was just so adrenaline- and panic-producing all at one time that I felt like now there was no alternative. I really just wanted to go back and finish my beer!

"I tried to time it so that I would jump when the water was at its highest point. But, instead, I waited too long, so the water was starting to recede again. That's when I chose to jump. So I wound up flying down at the same rate that the water was. So I actually hit the water when it was at its lowest point, not at its highest point. And I hit the water really hard on the side of my leg and it hurt like hell. And I went down into the water about twenty or thirty feet. But when I came to the surface, everyone was cheering. And I was thinking, *I did it! I did it!*

"I climbed up the ladder and somebody was going to give me a towel. But I went to the precipice and did it again, just to show that I could. And this time, I timed the water perfectly, so that it was about a sixty-foot jump. And it certainly hurt a lot less. And my pride was really strong. And I came out of there feeling that I had accomplished something truly important in my life," he said.

Years later, Michael would say, "That experience taught me that, even in the face of extreme fear and possibilities of danger, I learned the difference between taking just a leap of faith and taking a calculated leap of faith. From that point on, I have tried to focus on what I can control in any given situation, so as to make the risk a little more in my favor."

After Michael had returned home, he was able to apply this lesson from the road. "I recall a meeting where I was to give a significant presentation to land a huge account," Michael said.

"And it was different than any presentations I had ever given. And I remember thinking to myself, *Well you know you have this capability, even though you've never done this before. There have been lots of experiences where you've taken a calculated risk.* And I remember thinking about taking that calculated risk on the second dive in Jamaica.

"That experience has led to more of a change of my thinking," Michael said. "I don't conjure up an image of myself on the edge of that cliff whenever I'm about to take on a new experience that I'm afraid of. Instead, it's become more integrated into my psyche. When I am about to do something I haven't done before, I just know that I am the type of person who has built a series of successes in my life from trying things I haven't done before and getting good at them."

Courage is Faith Without Proof

Carol, a writer and editor with two grown children also learned about courage, while ascending a pyramid in Mexico alone.

Carol wrote to me that she once "decided blithely to climb the ninety-one steps of Chichen Itza." But, halfway up, she froze, with a paralyzing fear of heights. It felt like "the most frightening moment of my life," she said. "I was without help. No one would come and get me. I had to save myself."

Despite a "fear of heights that probably will always stay with me," Carol said, she did summit Chichen Itza, and has since scaled other pyramids in Mexico. And climbing those ancient steps taught Carol a critical lesson: "Courage is having faith in yourself when there is no proof that you deserve it."

Making the Right Decisions

I recently saw former New York City mayor, Rudy Giuliani, talk in Phoenix, and he spoke about courage. He described how life after 9/11 and his concurrent battle with cancer reminded him, "Courage is not the absence of fear. Courage is having fear and making the right decision anyway."

As Guiliani spoke, I thought about how some of us need to summon courage daily: to deal with difficult spouses, bosses, partners or companions; or to help battle illness, grief, loss, or tragedy. But, as Guiliani helped me realize, whatever the shape, when we summon courage and keep moving forward, despite our fears, we are able to embrace our experiences more fully. Courage enables us to live in the tide of our lives.

Choosing Courage

Mabel Dodge — hostess of the famous Greenwich Village salons, with such speakers as Emma Goldman, John Reed and Margaret Sanger — felt she was "atrophying" in New York.

She visited New Mexico in 1917, where she met her fourth and final husband, Tony Luhan, a Native American from Taos Pueblo. Mabel remained in Taos until her death in 1962.

Mabel Dodge Luhan believed that she and Tony were brought together for a reason. Her purpose for living, she said, was "to show how life may be, must be, lived."

Mabel and Tony's New Mexico home became a beacon for artists and writers. Guests included Georgia O'Keeffe, Ansel Adams, Willa Cather and D.H. Lawrence. Today the house is a popular bed-and-breakfast and a National Historic Landmark.

Mabel wrote five books about Taos: *Edge of Taos Desert,*

Los Gallos, Winter in Taos, Lorenzo in Taos, and *Taos and Its Artists.* Her stories evoked a life of riding horses with Tony in the hills, soaking in hot springs and letting her hair dry in the sun, hosting dinner parties, and Indians from the Pueblo dancing, singing and drumming in her living room. Her descriptions often read like a Frances Mayes book. I began to dream of living under the Taos sun.

Dodge Luhan possessed many qualities I chose not to dwell on. She interfered in people's lives, not always in their best interests. She often acted icy to people who did not engage her. Yet I was attracted to her for several reasons. Acquaintances in New Mexico said, "She enjoyed life more than anybody I know." Writer Carl Van Vechten said she had a tremendous appetite to "know" and experience "everything." Painter Dorothy Brett said Mabel had an "insatiable appetite for tasting life in all its aspects." Mabel's thirst for life intrigued me, but her courage inspired me.

Mabel Dodge Luhan's biographer, Lois Rudnick, said, even as a child, Dodge demonstrated "exhibitions of power, of prowess, and of courage." And in Taos, people who knew her, like D.H. Lawrence, quickly acknowledged such qualities in her.

Lawrence first visited Taos at Mabel's behest. She did not know the English author at the time, but considered him one of the greatest writers of the twentieth century. She pleaded with him to come; writing him numerous letters and even creating private visualizations about him. After moving to Taos and getting to know Mabel, Lawrence readily spoke of her "dauntlessness."

Dodge Luhan developed a personal mission in New Mexico: to help preserve the native culture. Though she knew no one, she introduced herself to this new culture the first time she visited Taos Pueblo: She carried oranges with her, as she'd heard that small gifts could ingratiate her to the people there. Then she began walking to the Pueblo every day, where she was invited into people's homes, people's lives. Later, Mabel assisted John Collier, a Commissioner of Indian Affairs, and helped ensure that the Pueblo culture did not lose its religious practices. She wrote articles about the native culture in local and regional newspapers and enlisted artists and writers, such as Lawrence, to create stories about the region.

I admired Mabel, pioneering across the country, knowing little about the land she would soon call home; and creating a life there that made a difference.

Today, Taos natives still remember her influence. On my journey, I would meet the Pueblo sheriff, who would tell me, "Mabel did a lot of good here. She paved the way for non-Indians and Indians to get along more. Before her, there wasn't much communication. She really opened things a lot."

Mabel also left a legacy of courage. After reading Dodge Luhan's *Edge of Taos Desert*, photographer Ansel Adams wrote to Mabel that she had found "a real way of life" there. He wrote, "You found it, even though it required ruthless action and decision…Your transition was effected in a mood of strength and inevitability, and it is going to help many another woman and man to 'take life with the talons' and carry it high."

Lois Rudnick described Mabel's influence on her granddaughter, Bonnie. "She learned from her grandmother's independence and her courage" and from Mabel's "always resilient enthusiasm for living," she said. And Bonnie talked of how her grandmother never let obstacles stop her. "More than that," Bonnie said, she "did not believe that anything really did exist that could stand in her way. She taught me to trust myself and keep on going forward with my eyes wide open."

Dodge Luhan discovered a new vitality in her adopted homeland. She arrived "atrophying," yet, as Susan Chambers Cook said in a public television documentary about Mabel, "When she moved to Taos, she finally found herself."

Taos helped heal Mabel. She openly spoke about its regenerative qualities. She also said an "invisible but powerful spirit hovered over Taos Valley."

As I ventured into her footsteps, I wondered: what do words like regenerative and powerful spirit really mean when they are connected to a place? And might a modern traveler still experience them?

Battling Ghosts ✒

I did not seek courage in my travels to Mabel's New Mexico, rather a retreat. And Mabel Dodge Luhan's house looked like a sanctuary. An adobe home in an Italian-style courtyard, with potted flowers in bloom, cottonwood trees flanking a nearby creek, and mountains rising in the distance — I thought this would be an ideal place for restful rejuvenation.

I reserved Mabel's bedroom for myself and lined her room's bookshelves with works by her contemporaries, such as D.H. Lawrence, Georgia O'Keeffe, and Freida Lawrence.

On my first day in Taos, I walked toward the Pueblo and stopped at a trading post, where I met Tony, the owner, a Pueblo man, with thick silver hair and work-etched hands. He told me that he had known Dodge Luhan. She used to shop there with Dorothy Brett and Freida Lawrence. When I mentioned that I was studying Mabel and staying at her home, Tony giggled gently and said, "You might talk to Mabel in the night there."

That night, swinging under a dark sky in Mabel's courtyard, the wind kicked up. The air felt strangely thick, like barometric pressure rising, and the darkness was enveloping.

The following day as I strolled through town, stopping to chat with residents about Mabel and her life there, people started telling me stories of Mabel's "reappearance": a Hispanic house-keeper, a gift-shop attendant, a museum executive, each had their own tale. Alice, one of the receptionists back at Mabel's B&B, recounted an incident that happened some years earlier and frightened a guest so much that she left the following day. "You know what?" Alice said, "Something didn't feel right here last night while I was on my shift. I was concerned. I even called from home this morning to see if everything was okay," she said.

I remembered the wind, the swing, and the strange, thick air. I did not believe in ghosts, but I listened.

Slowly, my security began to slip away. My cell phone had stopped working just after I had crossed the New Mexico border. My debit card had disappeared forty-eight hours after I had arrived at Mabel's. And, in a pasture where I photographed a stallion that resembled Mabel's horse, Charley, a beautiful Indian man, suddenly started cursing me loudly and kicking stones. Was he drunk? Demented? On drugs?

On my hurried walk back to the B&B, I remembered what a woman had told me en route to Taos. Soaking in a hot springs soda pool, under a blood-red sunset, the woman told me that she had traveled internationally and lived throughout America, but from the moment she'd arrived in New Mexico, she knew it was home. I asked if she had found any of the spiritual renewal people often claimed here. "This place helps balance you," she said. "But it really pushes you, forward and back, continuously thrusting you around. Then you realize that you can endure that, and that's how you find balance."

Back at Mabel's that evening, I headed to the B&B's solarium. This is what the receptionist called it when I asked about a good place to watch the sunset. She had suggested I sneak up to the guestroom, which featured dramatic 360-degree views. No one was staying there and I'd have the place to myself. It sounded like a great plan.

The solarium resembled a fire lookout tower, but grander. The womb of glass was spartan, with two beds, a wooden chair, a chest of drawers, hangers on a wall, and a long mirror. Two sets of towels were stacked neatly on a chest.

I felt tranquil there, and sat quietly in the small room for more than an hour.

Two hours later, however, when I returned to the solarium after dinner, a towel from the neat stack hung over the banister. And a previously closed window was now wide open. Yet the room was empty. And the receptionist insisted that no one else had visited there.

I felt edgy, unready to return to Mabel's bedroom. I walked to her reading room, hoping to retreat in books. But the B&B's caretaker entered moments later. We exchanged brief pleasantries, talked about the weather, and life in New Mexico. Then he suddenly started telling me about Susan (Kitty) O'Tero, a previous owner of Mabel's home. He described her vexing "struggle" with Mabel's ghost. But he could not remember how the tale ended. His story brought a knot of fear to my stomach.

In Mabel's bedroom, I now felt genuinely scared. *What was happening, and why? What next?* It seemed the stakes had risen every day. Before turning out the lights, I wrote in my journal: now, for the first time, to Mabel. "Please...be gentle with me." Then I snapped off the bedside lamp and watched the shadows from trees sway on the bedroom walls.

The next morning I drove to my scheduled ride at the stables by the Pueblo. A "spirit ride," as the stable owner, Sandy, with a gravelly smoker's laugh, called it. "Decide what you want to dump when you're in those mountains," she said when I arrived. "You know, problems, concerns. We say that God walks around these mountains with his sleeves rolled up."

Sandy's husband, Storm Star, was a Native American man, from the Pueblo. Many said he was also a horse whisperer. Storm Star was also "real intuitive about people," Sandy said. "He taught me to read people."

I told Storm Star and Sandy that I was an "okay" rider. Having ridden since I was a kid, I had learned not to oversell my riding abilities, as I didn't want a horse I couldn't handle. The rule had proven useful, as in nearly thirty years, I had never fallen from a horse.

Storm Star chose Seneca, a "real high-spirited" four-year-old colt, for me to ride.

As I prepared to ride, I tried to think of troubles, concerns back home. But I could only think of one thing I wanted to leave in those mountains. Whatever the spirit, this atrophying force that had seemed to stalk me on this trip, I wanted it to end.

My horse chomped at the bit as we filed out of the stables. Bernard, my native guide, and I rode in silence at first, as we ventured into the parched, stark desert. Pinion and cactus blanketed the mud-cracked terrain. The sun struck down with what Mabel had described as a "walloping heat."

Bernard then asked if I wanted to lope. I said I did, and tightened my reins.

Suddenly, a pack of dogs charged up to my horse. Seneca spooked, and bucked. I clamped his sides with my thighs. He reared a second, and then a third time; like a riptide. He made an abrupt left turn, thrusting me far to the right. Then he started to race. He wanted me off. I clutched the saddle horn. My arms began to tremble. On another turn, when the gravity grew overpowering, I thumped to the ground.

Bernard leapt off his horse. "Man, that was bad," he said. "Are you alright?"

"Yeah," I said, not entirely sure that I was. I watched our horses tear across the barren land, barn-bound.

Bernard helped me up and we began walking toward the barn, through the desert. I paused to pick a few cactus spines from the back of my jeans; beneath, my legs quivered like a sewing machine.

Back at the stables, after seeing what had happened, Storm Star asked if I wanted to ride again. I wasn't sure. I ambled into the ranch office, feeling a bit dizzy. "You alright?" Sandy asked. Her little white terrier then followed me inside and came to stand by me. "She wants to make sure you're okay," Sandy said.

My eyes welled up. One tear trailed down my cheek. I quickly brushed it away with my dusty hand. I didn't want Sandy to see me crying. I did not want to weaken now. A few minutes later, I asked Storm Star to saddle a horse for me.

Back on the trail, Bernard recounted the earlier scene: "That was really something, man! It was like they'd just opened the chute and you were riding that bronco. They would've rung the bell for you," he said. "You were on for eight seconds."

"Really? Well, that's cool," I said.

Still keyed up several minutes later, Bernard said, "Man, you were real lucky. If you'd come off when he was bucking, you could've been trampled. If your foot hadn't come clean out of that stirrup, you could've been dragged."

I started to visualize these scenarios, realizing how serious this could have been.

I asked Bernard if we could be silent for a while. I knew I needed some quiet time.

I took a long, deep breath. I focused on the cedar and sage trees that surrounded us, felt the strong sun on my shoulders and tried to sink into its stark light.

We continued our silence as we ascended a steep hill. Then we rested our horses under the shade of a tree. I listened to my horse's breathing, felt it settle into a gentle lull. Suddenly, a sense of peace washed over me, and I felt my struggle was over.

As Bernard and I approached the stables, he began a soliloquy that surprised me. "You know, you had one of the challenges of a lifetime today," he said. "I've never seen that happen here before, and I don't think it'll ever happen again. But you got back on and rode. Not everyone would have done that. You were really tested, but you stayed tough. And you overcame the challenge. Now you're even stronger," he said.

In that moment, I realized I *felt* stronger. And I wondered: *Did we need these challenges in life to show us that we can battle ghosts — even if they are only our own?*

Courage Builds as We Re-Live It

Back home, I realized this was one of the toughest trips I'd ever taken. I'd traveled alone to Kenya, Argentina, Peru, and many other countries. People had told me those trips were going to be really scary, dangerous. Yet I had driven just to the next state and had experienced my most frightening episode while on the road. I felt exhausted. The trip was meant to be a form of vacation, but I returned feeling I *needed* a vacation. Yet I also felt fueled from the experience, *bolder* than I'd felt in a long time: suddenly capable of accomplishing more, unwilling to succumb to fears, to be bullied, or to settle for less than my best. Now I challenged assumptions and confronted situations and people that I would not have previously. I fought for what I believed in as I had never before. *Knew* what I believed in as I hadn't for years. *Cared* in a new way. Suddenly all of the times I had backed down in the past felt foreign to me: as if they belonged to someone else.

Facing Fears to Follow Our Hearts

"Going to cover a war is not necessarily the 'right decision,' " Lisa wrote, "but it was a decision I knew I had to make or forever regret. I had always wanted to do it, I wanted to prove I could do it, and I wanted to make a difference as a journalist in a way I couldn't as a business reporter."

Lisa was "no stranger to fear." In the past, she'd "met secretly with Jewish dissidents in the Soviet Union and faced down tanks with university students during violent riots in Indonesia. Defied the military junta in Myanmar to get an interview with opposition leader Aung San Suu Kyi, fled from tear gas and water cannons after anti-government protests in Malaysia, and been arrested by Zambian police on false charges of being a South African spy."

Yet, "this time the fear I had was different," she said. "Part of me was terrified of going to the unknown, the Middle East, without speaking Arabic — as a woman and a Jew, all of it. I would have to have been stupid or brain dead not to have been scared. But I knew I had to conquer the demons of fear and just go, and that it would be okay. It *was* okay, but it was tough. It was also one of the most life-changing and enhancing experiences I'll ever have," she said. "So for me," she added, "courage has definitely not been the absence of fear. Often it's been conquering the fear enough to follow my heart."

Lisa, an American journalist with a strong track record in business reporting, traveled to Iraq in April 2003, but was uncertain whether she would even be able to secure work there as a political correspondent. Yet long before Iraq, Lisa had made bold moves in her travels.

Her first trial, alone and overseas, was in 1983. "I was twenty-one years old and in London to research my senior thesis on broadcasting over the Iron Curtain," she said. "Someone at the BBC suggested I go *behind* the Iron Curtain to see it for myself. That was an idea I had been trying not to have myself. But it was the first of many times I knew, despite my fear, I had to do something. The last time was going to Baghdad.

"Putting myself on fast forward, I went to the Polish Embassy in London and got a visa. Then I got a train ticket to Berlin, where I managed to find the next train to Warsaw. I arrived at the train station in Poland and had already looked up the one hotel for foreigners, Hotel Victoria. I took a taxi to the hotel and went to check in. I was shocked when I was told the price of the room; much more than I had imagined or could afford. I tried to call the U.S. Embassy, knowing that the ambassador was the father of a classmate of mine. He was the only contact I had in Warsaw.

I didn't have the right coins, couldn't figure out how to use the phone, didn't speak the language and couldn't afford the hotel. As I sat in the lobby, trying to figure out my next move, I was embarrassed when, suddenly, I started to cry.

"An American man came over and asked if I needed help. I sobbed and explained everything. He offered to get me a room, no strings attached. It was the first of many times I encountered the kindness of strangers who have saved my life. It could have been different, but I trusted my instincts enough to trust him. It turns out he was a Polish-born Jew who had fled to the U.S. and was back in Poland on business. He was 'kosher,' as they say. My parents later telephoned him in Orange, New Jersey, to thank him for helping their daughter in a far-off place. He said he would have hoped someone would have helped his daughter in the same situation.

"The next day he introduced me to his long-time Polish friends, a female journalist, Helena, and her teenage son, Artur. They invited me to stay with them in their home. Artur was an aspiring journalist. I told him I wanted to meet Lech Walesa. He traveled with me on a train to Gdansk. We went to the shipyards and waited for Walesa to come out to a hero's welcome. Then I found a TV crew from ABC News. I persuaded them to take us with them to Walesa's house. Once there, we rang the bell and Artur told Danuta, Walesa's wife, that I was a student who had come all the way from America to meet her husband. She let us in. I interviewed Lech Walesa when he was still a dissident leader and used it in my thesis.

"More than the academic coup, though," Lisa said, "was the personal triumph. I had gone by myself into the unknown, met a historic leader and made friends for life.

"I always look back on that whenever I am in trouble and think, *You found Lech Walesa, you can do xxx.* In fact, (and unfortunately!) it is something my mother always uses on me when I say I can't do something. It is an experience that still, more than twenty years later, manifests in my daily life."

And Lisa did work in Baghdad. She became one of the longest-serving American reporters in the war in Iraq.

Finding Fuel for Courage from the Past

Lisa's older sister, Laura, also a writer, has faced her own challenges, yet in a very different way. As she wrote to me:

"Many years ago, in my sixteenth summer, I contracted a chronic illness and left *normal* behind, but, during the summer before that one, when freedom and flexibility and fortune were still mine, I traveled to Italy and France with my family and, while there, I gathered memories that, although I didn't know it at the time, I would carry with me, like tokens of Before, through all the darkness that was waiting just ahead. There have been times in these years since when I have veered dangerously close to loss — of the use of my limbs, of my laughter and light, of all that I had thought of as my life — but, through all those times, those memories have never lost their hold on me.

"Look: There I am, sitting in the waiting room of a radiology lab where I, by now, have waited countless times before — to be called in for x-rays, for CT scans, for MRIs, for ultrasounds — peering out from above the indignity of a green, open-backed gown, watching the future I'd memorized long ago (as if I had been promised, and had not merely desired, it) become as faint and unsure as a photograph removed prematurely from developing fluid. I'm glancing over the top of a *Newsweek* at the people waiting on the chairs along the opposite wall, with a growing sense of awareness that here, within this room, desire no longer matters. There are no complaint forms to fill out, no voting booths to enter; there are no opinion polls. 'I see,' is written in each of the sets of eyes lined up before me. '*This* is where Life has decided to bring me to now.' And so I close my own eyes and reach into my store of memories for one of those tokens, as I might reach into my pocket to wrap my fingers around the comfort of a worry stone...

"...and, at once, I am again *in a tucked-away courtyard in Venice, eating* zuppa de pesce *with my family at an outdoor café, with children chasing a kickball across the cobblestones and church bells ambering in the dying twilight and women leaning out over the ancient window sills where women have leaned for centuries, calling their families home. There are men tipped back in their chairs at a table near ours, lifting their glasses to the rising moon, and a stream of lovers strolling past us, their bodies intertwined, and, from somewhere off in the distance come the velvet voices of gondoliers, dipping and soaring, tremoring and swelling, embroidering the night. The air smells of garlic and of garbage, of history and of heat, and, every time I inhale it, I see the summer stretched out ahead, as filled with promise and possibility as a gift-wrapped package waiting to be opened, so that breathing it — even in memory, these many years later — I feel a shiver of anticipation and, with it, perfect peace.*

"Or I am again *taking a sunset stroll through the winding back roads of an Italian hill town, coming upon the mother and her baby, also out for a stroll, whom I have carried along with me through all these years since I first saw them then. There they are, standing in the shadow of a row of cypress trees not far from their rustic stone house, visiting with the neighbors whom they have happened upon in the dusk as the first faint spray of sapphire stars is just beginning to emerge through the clouds overhead and the last golden light is dissolving from that point in the distance where the olive groves meet the sky. That baby certainly has babies of her own by now, but, in my mind, she will always be a baby herself, cradled forever in that lavender moment when she sat back on her mother's hip with evening gathering in softness around her and summer fragrant in the blossoms above, and I know that what I hold there, in that memory snapshot, is a vision of what I thought the world would always be, a vision of who I was at that moment, filled with certainty and hope.*

"Or I am again *sitting on a bench with my grandmother alongside the Seine, early on a misty morning, sharing a bag of steaming croissants which we're pulling apart with our fingers (releasing their buttery aroma to bloom in the air), and watching the parade of Parisians who are hurrying past us, beginning their day. I'm deep in conversation with her — about how she sat on the banks of the Thames with her grandmother when she was a small girl in London, and about what we'll do with this morning once my parents and sisters finish dressing and come down from our hotel, and about whether or not we should share our croissants with those pigeons who have clustered at our feet — but, even as I'm listening and laughing and watching and talking, the thought is coming to me at that moment that, when I'm home again, across the world, this will still be here: this river, silvering here before me beneath the slant of light from a marble sky, and those bateaux mouches silking, queenlike, along it, their foghorns a bass note in the city's song, and the Pont Neuf, pirouetting across it, and those apartment buildings there on its opposite bank, their ivory façades tinted rose by the sun, and all of the families inside them who are going about the everyday business of stumbling to their showers and buttoning their blouses and finishing their breakfasts and hunting for their shoes. The thought is coming to me at that moment that, even when I'm back on the other side of the ocean, doing those routine things in my own world, they will be right here, where I will have left them, doing them, too — and, in that instant, the world becomes an infinitely more intimate place for me and I, in it, forever less alone.*

Although life has since taught me other, more painful, lessons, and although a technician will, at any moment, step into the waiting room and call my name, wrenching me back to the bleached and sterile present of this ominous radiology lab, they are mine to keep forever, those moments-ripened-to-memories, the mesmerizing spells they cast back then made all the more magical by the solace they now bring."

❧

Step into Your Courage

1. *Adopt a local hero.* Ask native people whom they admire and deem courageous in their country's history. Explore this new entry point to the place you are visiting, a landmark on your own path to courage.

2. *Go solo.* Tap your courage and possibly gain a more intimate experience of the destination you are visiting.

3. *Bring your "road courage" back home.* Revisit those pivotal moments when you were at the precipice of your own cliff, ready to dive.

Chapter 8

Live an Abundant Life

"I WANT MY TOMBSTONE TO READ, 'He Paid Attention,'" Bruce said, as I sat in his office one afternoon. Bruce also recalled one of his "Ah ha! moments" of travel that afternoon: visiting Hearst Castle in San Simeon, three years earlier.

Bruce is one of the more "abundant" people I know. He runs a thriving e-commerce business, which he loves discussing, but speaks with equal passion about antique cars, art, good wine, books, music, new ideas, travel, tennis, poetry slams, museums, relationships, family and the meaning of things. Bruce sees the bounty in life and reaches for it.

On his first trip to Hearst Castle, he went with his fiancé, to whom he had proposed the day before. "I had never been," Bruce said, "although, because of my publishing background, I was certainly very aware of William Randolph Hearst, and I had read a biography of him. But the biography focused on his business and Hollywood activities, and a bit about what an S.O.B. he was. I certainly had heard about Hearst Castle and that Hearst had built it over many, many years and that, during his heyday, he entertained many Hollywood celebrities there."

But one background detail particularly impressed Bruce. "The genesis of Hearst Castle was that when Hearst was ten years old his mother whisked him off for a year-long European trip. They visited the capitals of Europe and the Middle East and, because of her interest in art and her fine education, it was just an amazing total immersion into European art, history, literature, etc. first-hand," Bruce said. "So he came home and basically devoted his entire life to bringing as many art treasures as possible from the rest of the world and concentrating them in this one place that he was building."

And from the moment that Bruce began touring Hearst Castle, he was "overwhelmed."

"Everywhere you go in this Byzantine area of the castle grounds, every corner you turn, every step, every square inch is replete with urns from ancient Greece, frescoes from Rome, ceilings from ancient Italy and other places in Europe, and phenomenal, just phenomenal, tapestries, and furniture from all over the world. And the *abundance* of this stuff: warehouses of the castle hold more stuff than the castle itself. Hearst basically went on a lifetime shopping spree.

"I'm sure somebody who goes to garage sales and auctions would think this was the Holy Grail. He really was a man who loved beautiful historic antiquities, who had the wherewithal and the interest to collect them, and who had the opportunity to build this palace to house them. You put it all together, and it is a truly unique, Shangri-La place."

The castle so impressed Bruce that he returned there two times that week and has visited since.

"The Hearst Castle is potentially a transformative place for travel," Bruce said, "because if you go there and are open and receptive — you don't have to go with any knowledge — you can then go to a lot of other parts of the world and appreciate what, say, twelfth century ceilings are all about; which I did, come to think, last year when I was in Burgundy. I was staying in a house built in the 1100s and looking at the same sort of ceilings.

"Seeing a lot of the European arts and antiquities in their natural habitat, seeing the *Hospice de Beaune*, and all of the beautiful woodwork and metalwork and ceilings…I absolutely know, having spent several trips to Hearst Castle, that my appreciation of some of the woodwork, and the ceilings, and the architecture is greater than what it would have been had I not been there.

"That's the thing: it's a sampler pack of arts and antiquities around the world, and you get to see it in its real setting. This is all in context," he said. "That's always been one of the jobs of the museum — to give people an up-close-and-personal touch of a lot of other things in the world they may never get to experience first-hand."

Bruce went on to mention other memorable travels in his life, including a journey to the South Pole just out of college while working as a journalist for the *Navy Times*. He traveled on a three-week press and diplomatic tour of Antarctica with daily newspaper writers from some of the biggest papers in the world. There was also the Civil War battles trip he created with his two sons. But what impressed me most is that Bruce, in his late fifties, having seen, experienced, and acquired much in his life, still had an almost childlike wonder about his travel to the Hearst Castle; and he had become further enriched and perhaps even touched by transformation there.

After discussing the South Pole, Bruce returned to talk of the Hearst Castle, and again, alluded to its transformative potential. "The Hearst Castle is an experience that anybody who pays their $10.95, or whatever it is, can have, if they pay attention," Bruce said. "If they make the trip, and they pay attention."

Yes, that's right: it's about paying attention.

Uncovering "Life More Abundant"

Wouldn't you love to feel a spirit of abundance daily? We often think that abundance means financial wealth. Certainly that is an aspect of abundance, but our riches are more bountiful than that. At the end of his travel book about Greece, *The Colossus of Maroussi*, Henry Miller said, "I refuse categorically to become anything less than the citizen of the world which I silently declared myself to be when I stood in Agamemnon's tomb. From that day forth my life was dedicated to the recovery of the divinity of man. Peace to all men, I say, and life more abundant!"

I believe that Miller tapped some of his spirit of abundance through paying attention; seeking "the divinity of man," always expecting "everything of the world," and being ready to "give everything." And from following his own advice to "Develop interest in life as you see it," Miller said, "in people, things, literature, music — the world is so rich, simply throbbing with rich treasures, beautiful souls, and interesting people. Forget yourself."

Finding "Rich Treasures, Beautiful Souls"

"There were a couple of times in our travels when I found a bond with women of different cultures, so that our similarities were more connecting than our differences," Rochelle, a novelist and mother of three grown daughters, said.

"The first was in Turkey when we were in Konya, in the museum of the Whirling Dervishes. I had been starting to feel sick to my stomach on my way to the museum. And, by the time we got maybe a half-hour into the museum, I knew I had serious stomach upset, and that was not unusual. In Turkey, much of the food you eat is out on buffet. The night before, I had eaten yogurt not out of a carton but from a bowl. And I thought, *Ah ha! That's what I did to myself.*

"I really got an urgent need to find a woman's room," Rochelle said. "There was an enormous crowd in the museum, milling around. It was a holiday, a Muslim holiday, and this was a Muslim neighborhood, so there was this huge crowd, and I couldn't even find my husband. But I saw a couple of people from our group and our instructions were to wander through the museum and meet at such an hour. Knowing I might not find my husband, and knowing I couldn't take much time looking for him, I told a couple of people in the group, 'Look, I will meet you at the bus. Don't leave without me.' And I left the museum, not knowing where I was going, but I kept asking, 'Toilet, Toilet,' and people kept pointing.

"And finally, in a courtyard — there was a series of courtyards and benches and fountains and parks — was clearly a woman's washroom. But there was a man sitting at the door, taking coins — as is the case all over Turkey. Well, I had left my purse on the bus because the tour guide said, 'Leave your purse here. It's going to be locked up, and you don't want to go in that crowded museum and risk getting your passport or money lifted, etc.' So, I had nothing with me except myself and an urgent need for a bathroom.

"When I tried to get into the bathroom, the man sitting outside the door started screaming at me, in Turkish, but I was not to be stopped. I went right in. He couldn't follow me; there is strict separation of the sexes there. I went into a stall and did what I had to do. I really was sick," Rochelle said.

"And when I came out, I must have looked white or yellow or beige. The women who were milling around the area where you wash your hands took one look at me, did not ask me a question, and led me to the sink. They washed my hands, then washed my face. Then they led me to a little puddle with a small fountain running. Told me to take my shoes off, because in the stall there was no more than a hole in the ground and you had to squat. Then they washed my feet. Then one of them brought out a comb and combed my hair. And they just patted me and toweled me. And then one of them sort of held me to her chest, which felt awfully good. And then they walked me out of there.

"They didn't know exactly what had happened but they could guess, they sort of inferred. And they were making small Muslim sounds. I wasn't saying anything except, 'Thank you, thank you, thank you.' Then they walked me past the man at the gate, who was gunning for me, still wanted to know where his coins were. And one of them dropped coins and hollered something at him, which cowed him. He was properly admonished. Then they pointed me in the direction of the museum, and I finally found my way back to the tour bus.

"I was so astonished by what had happened. I thought what they did was so tender, and kind, and so necessary, because I was just a bundle of misery. And these women didn't know me from Adam. They just knew that I was probably American, and, not waiting to hear what had afflicted me, nor who I was, just took to comforting me in the way that big, maternal women do. I felt I had found a sisterhood of women that knew what I needed at that time," Rochelle said, "and it had nothing to do with where we had come from."

This experience has reverberated in Rochelle's life. Since her time in Turkey, she has encountered other affirming experiences with women in her travels: from writers' conferences in America to subsequent journeys overseas. As a result, she feels that moving through the world "seems less scary, because you know that, wherever you go, you find groups of women; that there is going to be some kind of shelter, if you need it."

When Life Makes You Drunk

Best known for his more "sexual" works, such as *The Tropic of Cancer* and *The Tropic of Capricorn*, Henry Miller had a spiritual awakening in Greece that changed his life forever. Erica Jong said in her insightful book about Miller, *The Devil at Large*, when Miller went to Greece, "He was almost fifty, and ready to enter the next phase of his life." And "He returned to America a new person," she said. "In a sense, his soul had been shriven."

In Greece, Miller discovered a new way of seeing, a new way of being. As he wrote in *The Colossus of Maroussi*, "The light of Greece opened my eyes, penetrated my pores, expanded my whole being." Friend, lover, and fellow author Anaïs Nin would say that Miller was "a man whom life makes drunk." Erica Jong also experienced Miller's infectious vitality. After years of Miller's mentorship and friendship, Jong said that Miller was "more alive than most people ever are, and when you were near him, he shed his light and life force on you."

Miller cultivated this abundant spirit, Jong said, through various means: "Sex was one path toward abundance. Travel, another. Conversation, letter-writing, and painting were still others," she wrote.

As I stepped out onto Henry Miller's path, I wondered whether I would find my own road to abundance.

Dream-Weaving

When I departed for Greece, I was at a crossroads. I had worked at my job in public television for almost eleven years and enjoyed it. I felt comfortable there. Yet I also had started to feel a gnawing need for change. People at the station often stayed there twenty, thirty, or forty years — until they were ready to retire. Every logical part of me said it was foolish to forego such security.

Yet I had a long-time dream. A dream I had yearned to dive into, but it was as if I was in The Blue Grotto, and could not discard my swimsuit.

When I arrived in Henry Miller's Greece, I had only one desire: to better understand "life more abundant." What did it really mean? And how might it apply to my life?

I based myself in one of Miller's favorite places, the island of Poros. He described his journey that began there: "There is only one analogy I can make to explain the nature of this voyage which began at Poros and ended at Tripolis perhaps two months later...It was a voyage into the light," Miller said. While I was on the island, I also learned that *poros* in Greek means "passages."

I took day trips from Poros. And, toward the end of my sojourn, visited Mycenae, the ruins of one of the greatest cities of the Mycenaean civilization, which dominated part of the

Mediterranean world from the fifteenth to twelfth century B.C.

At a well on the site, I remembered how Miller had encountered some of his own demons there. His friend, Katsimbalis — the "Colossus of Maroussi" — desperately wanted to go down the well, but Miller refused. Even when he returned with his old friends the Durrells, Miller refused to go. He would not venture "into that slimy well of horrors," he said. "Not if there were a pot of gold to be filched."

But I felt compelled to step into the darkness. Two young men walked before me to the mouth of the cave, then stopped. I entered the well alone, unsure how far I would go. I only knew that I had to go. Go deep. Feel afraid. Keep moving. Embrace the unknown.

As I traveled deeper, the walls felt damp, the stairs slick. I could see nothing. I could only offer a blind dance in the dark. Slowly, I would slide one foot across each stone stair, to the lip, then dangle it to the step below. My stationary foot would follow.

I continued this dance until a pencil-thin light appeared from behind. A young woman had started the journey as well. She wore a tiny headlamp.

Together, we tread carefully to the cistern floor.

As we ascended, I still felt anxious, yet jubilant. I had explored somewhere one of my literary heroes had refused; a first, I imagined. I also decided to believe that this woman's appearance offered a message: *If we step boldly into the unknown, our path may become illuminated.*

As I continued to stroll through the grounds of Mycenae, I realized now what I needed to do. I had entered into the cave. I had touched the walls for good luck. Now I needed to shuck my swimming suit and dive in.

Ever since my first trip to Europe as a teenager, travel had become a consuming passion for me. It was the subject that would keep me reading, dreaming at night, and the prospect of which would stir me in the morning.

I had loved producing travel documentaries in my public television job. Before that, I had done the same out of London for several years. But now I dreamed of living my passion for travel daily.

On my last full day in Poros, I visited a nearby church. Inside, two Greek orthodox priests sang. The bearded men wore black capes and long white scarves that flowed down their flanks like table runners. A boy in street-clothes chanted after the black-bearded priest. A mentally-impaired girl about nine years old, with wide, dark eyes and frizzy, brown hair that framed her face, stood smiling, profusely, throughout: first at me, facing me, four feet away. Then at the priest, standing squarely before him. Her mother tried to distract the young girl, discourage her. But she persisted. Smiling throughout, in boundless, beautiful fascination. Although she was "handicapped," the girl's breathless joy illuminated the room: exalted it.

Gilded frescoes of religious scenes colored the church walls. Light poured through the windows — reflecting yellow and blue, the hues of the panes. The wind howled and the sea crashed outside. The church door remained open: everything open. A vagrant dog wandered in and paced along the back pews. And, while I had never considered myself a religious person, for the first time ever, I sensed a spiritual presence, which felt almost palpable: in the wind, in the sea, in the light streaming through, in the vagabond dog and in the "simple" girl full of wonder, in the singing priest, swinging his thurible of incense throughout the church, and to all of us in it.

Flying back to America, I realized that I had glimpsed Miller's "voyage into the light." Now it was time to create my own "life more abundant," and take a giant leap. Three months later, I resigned from my job, to follow my dream.

Finding Abundance of Spirit

"It was an everyday scenario," Jeremy wrote. "Youthful travelers surrounded by family and friends at Sydney Airport as they set off on the 'Grand Tour.' But few Grand Tours are accompanied with musical instruments and a modicum of finances. Our plan was to survive, prosper and learn on the road. We would be buskers. Professional entertainers who would fund our journey through our trade. Learn about countries and cultures from the street level up. See the real Europe through a year of great change and no small amount of hope," he said.

"Not only would we have adventures with people and places and food, we would acquire knowledge on what to busk, where, when, how, and for how long. There were police and conmen. Fellow musicians and promoters. Tourists and locals, music lovers alike. There were the major sights and the obscure details. We slept in hotels, houses and parks. We saw the continent outside of the tourist buses, youth hostels and art galleries. We saw those too, but most of all, we immersed ourselves in the seething pot of humanity and found it a comfortable and desirable stew. It was our 'time of gifts,' our 'rite of passage.' Life was the aim, with music as the tool."

Jeremy continued, "Genoa would represent a turning point, though we didn't realize it at the time. We had lived off the busking up until then, and even though we were going through some lean times, it was nothing that a hard, profitable set wouldn't fix."

Yet, the group had committed to hotel rooms they couldn't afford and had spent a long day seeking a spot with ample crowds to busk for, yet had found none.

"As it neared dinnertime, the hunger in our bellies was aching to be abated," Jeremy said. "It was then that we realized our position. First, we needed to eat before joining the 'hustings' again. Second, we were not in possession of a great deal of *lire*. Third, we had to make enough cash to pay for the hotel rooms. Fourth, much the same conditions would need to be faced again tomorrow.

"In fact, it would not be dishonest to say that, for the first time in my life, I was really hungry and was too skint to do anything about it. Sure, there was always the 'plastic' or traveler's checks, but it was not an option for all of us. Besides, we had a job to do and backing out now would be to admit defeat. The money would probably only last a few weeks, then we'd have to go home. Back to the comfortable shores of middle-class life in Sydney. A bunch of pathetic failures. Only lasting three months.

"Grimly, we soldiered on. And, eventually, we turned a corner and saw an open bar with at least ten people in attendance. This oasis to our weary eyes was obviously not the complete answer to our dreams. But we could reason that, where there is one bar, one can perhaps find another and yet another. If we could find ten such bars, we could earn enough to get us through this evening's imbroglio. A tall order, but at least it now seemed vaguely possible.

"So we set to work: wiping the look of desperation from our faces, we reverted to the smiling mien of musical entertainers and adjusted our postures accordingly. It was not the time to ask permission; simply enter the fray and hope for the best.

"We started low, trickling into our opening instrumental melody and creeping across the road as one unit. As it turned out, the patrons were pleased, and after a few songs, the hat was passed around and remuneration was forthcoming.

"Reasonably happy that we had made a start, we turned to leave and tread the path of exploration once more; but were halted by exhortations from behind the bar. Though we had virtually no understanding of the Italian language, it seemed obvious that the manager wished that we would stay and play awhile.

"The manager talked to us at length in his native tongue, which was lost on us. Finally, he got one of the guys there, who spoke French, to translate to me what he was trying to say, whereupon I would confer with the others in the group. This struck me as dangerous, not only because translating across a number of languages could create misinformation, but also because my understanding of French was far from adequate. We pressed on regardless. The conversation took at least twenty minutes, but the gist of it was this:

The manager wanted us to stay and play.

Out of the question, we affirmed.

We were offered free drinks to keep performing.

A lovely offer, we replied, but we need to earn some more money.

He was prepared to pay us some *lire* if we hung around.

We responded that it was a kind proposal, but we needed to make enough money to pay for our hotels that evening.

How much, he wanted to know?

We informed him.

No problem, plus he would give us a lift back in his car.

It was too good to be true.

"We looked at each other with a mixture of joy and relief that was increased as the first beer was passed over the bar. If we were religious types, we would have given thanks. I think we gave thanks anyway.

"Come the morning, we met at the train station nice and early. For us, that meant around nine-thirty. We had decided to head to Rapallo, but a train didn't leave for a couple of hours. Since the meager sum required for the tickets basically cleaned us out of all liquid currency, it was determined that those of us with instruments should head back into the shopping district and busk up some pocket money.

"This was not what I wanted to hear. I was definitely in one of those let's-just-get-out-of-town moods. As far as I was concerned, the place had slapped us around, and then, very magnanimously, let us off the hook at the last minute. It seemed unwise to tempt fate by hanging around. Why not just cut our losses and start life afresh in a new world, unfettered by the emotional baggage of the last twenty-four hours?

"Whether these feelings were transmitted to the others or not, I can't be sure. Suffice to say, we had to wait around anyway and it was generally felt that we could do ourselves no harm and could only gain from trying our luck on the morning's traffic.

"We were playing with verve as we normally did at the beginning of a set," Jeremy continued. "Smiling and jumping up and down, we noticed that we were attracting a small crowd fairly quickly. Even before the end of the first number, a couple of thousand-*lire* notes found themselves floating into the bottom of the guitar case.

"Then, around the second or third song something happened. It's not an easy thing to explain, but the crowd quickly built up and affected us to an extraordinary degree. There were suddenly about twenty or thirty people, and they were really enjoying the music. This abruptly had the effect of kicking us into an extra gear that we weren't sure we had.

"I distinctly remember looking around, seeing the unbridled joy on the faces of those watching us play, then making eye contact with everyone in the band as we recognized that the force of the audience's delight was inspiring in us a performance that felt the music inside and out, effortlessly playing and singing with a gusto that enveloped and lifted us a foot or two off the ground.

"The crowd swelled like an organic beast. Undulating around its edges, people broke off to flick thousand-*lire* notes into the case.

"To our right, the door to a café bar swung open and a man in a white smock came dancing out balancing a tray, upon which rested a bottle of spumante and four fluted glasses. This brought a cheer from the assembled masses as he placed it in the guitar case.

"Not to be outdone, the proprietor of a fruit shop across the square came charging out, swaying his hips to the music and balancing a large box of fruit above his head. To even more roars from the crowd, he deposited it on top of the case, the pineapple and other sizable goodies making it too large to fit inside.

"Again, we all looked at each other, uncomprehendingly reveling in our reversal of fortune; in this typical Italian *joie de vivre,* or, if you prefer, in this *dolce vita.*

"We could do nothing else but play on as the rattle of coins and the rustle of paper performed a sweet melody of their own to our weary ears.

"Then, suddenly, we realized that our train was departing in less than half an hour. We finished up the set, thanked the crowd, who, good-naturedly, let us go. And the proprietor cracked open a bottle of bubbly while my friend, Peter, and I divvied up the income. Flushed with spumante and the excitement of playing an awesome set, we hotfooted it back to the station, juggling the instruments and our new-gotten gains, laughing all the way. The experience we'd just had filled us with an unbeatable lust for life.

"After everything that happened," Jeremy wrote me later, "it was impossible to think of Genoa with mixed feelings. There was only complete elation. The place drove us down to the depths, then saved and lifted us to dizzying heights that we hadn't even considered before. Looking back, I realize the Genoa incident was indicative of our busking trip as a whole. It ingrained in all of us the belief that people are fantastic. The generosity of friendship, food and shelter that we were offered everywhere was in equal measure to the monetary rewards," Jeremy, now a film director and editor, said. "We always met people with open hearts."

The Practice of Gratitude

"Everyone gets into rock 'n' roll for the girls. If they don't confess that, they're lying," Billy, a professional musician, said. "But, for me, it became as much about the travel. Travel has changed my life beyond my wildest imagination.

"I have been on every continent, save Australia," he continued. "I was in Moscow with Chuck Berry. I was the Pointer Sisters' Tour Manager and went to the Middle East with them."

In Egypt, Billy would learn a lesson that would shape him today.

"When I was in Cairo with the Pointer Sisters, their manager, who was gay, said, 'Meet me in the lobby at eleven tonight and wear a jacket.' I thought he was going to drag me to all these gay bars, that he'd want to go carousing," Billy said. "I didn't want to go and was feeling disgruntled. Not that there was anything wrong with that, but that wasn't my thing."

Billy reluctantly agreed to go, however, and showed up at the appointed time. Instead of taking him to gay bars, the manager had "arranged to go on a camel ride at midnight at the Pyramids!" Billy said. "This wasn't something many people got to do. And, after a little while, we stopped and laid out a blanket. I could hear the berbers singing in high voices in the distance. And I sat watching the moonrise over the Sphinx. And it was one of those complete magic moments," Billy said. "And I thought, this is why I became a musician. This is what rock 'n' roll has done for me.

"I realized you don't get many opportunities to get *paid* to do this kind of thing," Billy said. "I had a moment of clarity, a feeling of great gratitude. And since that time, it's been like a muse over my shoulder that says, 'Remember this. Savor this: This lucky moment, this magic moment. You can't take it with you.'

"I've almost made my own small practice of gratitude since," Billy said. "No matter where life has taken me, I often remember that moment with the moon rising over the Pyramids, and the Sphinx, and feeling, *My gosh, what great fortune I've had.* And that's what gets you through the tough times: those moments when you become a better – if not better, then more enlightened – person. Everybody has their own purgatory they need to deal with. We all have our own mountains we need to climb. This has helped me climb mine."

Becoming One of the Wealthiest People in the World

"That is one thing about travel," Ellen said. "I learned a lot about how I present myself in the world, who I am in the world, and who I am to others. It's like, 'Ooh, What do you do for a living? Are you married or single? Do you have kids?' And, when we were traveling, people would say, 'What do you do?' And I said, 'Well, I'm traveling. I'm seeing the world.' Then, when we stopped traveling, I felt like, *Now how do I define myself?* I had to do some soul searching to figure that out."

Ellen came from parents who had followed dreams and discovered abundance on the road. "I think the sailing trip saved my dad's life," Ellen said. "You should ask him about that." So I did. The following day, Ellen's father told me, "Oh yes, I was getting very uptight in my job. And I think that, if I had continued in that job, I probably would've ended up with a heart attack. I think I was a Type A, and things weren't going the way I wanted them to go, and so I figured, well, I can't change them. The only one I can change is myself. So I said, 'Okay, I'm leaving,' " Joe said. "And that's what I did."

"Joe had always read pirate stories as a kid and dreamed of sailing" Joe's wife, "Mo," told me. But Mo did not share this fantasy. Yet she knew she wanted to help her husband live his dream.

Joe's dream turned into the couple's seven-year sailing expedition around the Caribbean. They described how one of the greatest joys of their passage was seeing how warm, embracing and helpful people they met from around the world were. "Every place we went the people were just wonderful," Joe said. Mo quickly added, "Yes, they were outstandingly nice."

Following in her parents' footsteps, Ellen, and her husband, Gary, would strike out on their own path of dreams. Ellen was in her late twenties and Gary almost forty. They "got a little truck with a shell on the back of it and traveled the states for eight months, and camped," she said. "We drove around and saw Mt. Rushmore and Yelllowstone and visited family and friends.

"We left with very little money," she said. "Two thousand dollars in cash. We had our bicycles, camping gear, stuff to cook with and two plastic camp chairs. And that was all we had. And we figured that, if we couldn't make it, we'd come back to California and go to work.

"We wanted to see if we could travel the country, help out friends, help out family, and just make ourselves available, looking for opportunities to contribute – what would happen?"

Quickly, Ellen and Gary started seeing the answer. "It seemed everywhere we went it was open doors," she said. "It was so welcoming. I think some of it had to do with our attitude; looking for ways to contribute, or add, to people's lives."

So, I asked, what was one of the biggest contributions they made?

"We were awake and available to have conversations with people," she said. Sometimes it was as simple as cooking a pesto dinner with French bread and a bottle of wine on the beach for people who had helped them when their car broke down, and the group ended up talking through the night. For others, it was seeing that you aren't trapped. "You can be free," Ellen said. "You don't have to do what you're doing; if you don't like it. If it's not agreeable to you. If where you're living isn't working. If how you're living isn't working. If who you're living with isn't working. You aren't stuck. You can make changes. And you don't have to have all the money in the world to go and do something different. And you don't have to have it all set up ahead of time," she said. "Gary very much operates out of faith. That is, if we're available and looking for ways to contribute, we'll be taken care of in the process."

Ellen found many gifts while on the road, but one came in a surprising guise. "We ended up being broke at one point, and decided we'd just head back to California," she said. "We stopped at some friends' house in Tennessee. They'd had a freeze while they were out of town. The entire area had had a freeze and a lot of people ended up with broken water pipes and flooding. Our friends needed to have their house fixed, but couldn't get anyone to come fix it, because all these other people were in the same situation, and contractors could pick and choose who they wanted to work for.

"We had stopped at their house on the way to California and they asked us if we'd do construction for them," Ellen said, "and that turned my life around. I had never done construction, but Gary had. We stayed for three months and repaired the damage, and then we remodeled their house. In the process, I learned construction, and I learned that I loved construction. I have my own construction business now," she shared.

Yet Ellen's greatest reward from their eight-month journey was it "gave us time to be with family and friends and have relationships that were deep," she said. Ellen and Gary were able to "show up" and contribute to the lives of people they loved.

Ultimately, this gift also would help Ellen through hard times. At forty, Ellen began seriously questioning, "What do you have to show for your life? What have you accomplished?" She encountered a personal crisis. A friend then recounted one comment Oprah Winfrey had made during a speech she had given at a women's convention. Ellen said, "This one thing he told me turned my life around."

Her friend recalled that Oprah had spoken about, "You know,

everybody judges each other. But she said when you die, this is what's going to be important — It's not going to be what color your car was, what kind did you drive, how fat or thin were you, how big was your house, what kind of job did you do — What's going to matter in the end is: who did you love, and who loved you?

"That's what matters," Ellen said. "Who did you love? And at the time it felt even more so to me who did you love? *Who did you get to love?* Suddenly that's when I felt like I was one of the wealthiest people in the world. I felt so blessed, and so wealthy — in love."

Paying It Forward

"When I graduated from business school, my mother wanted to buy me a fancy watch. And I didn't want one," Peter said. "I said I wanted to take a trip. My mother was opposed to the trip. My father supported it. My mom said she wanted to give me something I would remember forever. My father said, 'If we send him on this trip, he will remember it forever.' "

Peter, now a successful financial manager, would travel for six weeks, mostly alone, through Central and East Africa. And, while in Tanzania, he joined a group for part of the trip. "There were two drivers in our group," Peter said, "one of them was named Mohammed. I was the only single person, so I got to be sort of friendly with this guy. And one of the first days we were in a real town, Mohammed said, 'Let's go have a drink.' I said, 'Oh, you're Muslim, you don't drink.' And he said, 'You're Jewish, do you eat pork?' And I said, 'Sometimes.' And he said, 'Well, I'm Muslim and I've been known to have a drink.'

"So we became thick friends in a very short amount of time,"

Peter said. "And, at the end of the trip, I was going to have this layover in Nairobi and Mohammed invited me to come home with him.

"So I got to spend thirty-six hours in a village, in a real Masai village. I was welcomed by his family. I slept on the ground. I ate what they ate. I drank what they drank. There was a pretty big celebration, having an outsider there. I was fascinated. I would've gone lion hunting with the kids if they had let me. I sat next to the village elder, who spoke not a lick of English, because it was my place of prominence as a guest. I ate a goat meat stew that was so spicy — and I like spicy foods — that my eyes were running, and, ultimately, I got so violently ill that you don't even want to know about it. I also drank this special homemade honey wine that was like a hallucinogenic. It was spiritual. The whole experience was very, very spiritual," Peter said.

Why was it so spiritual?

"These people have no real commerce, no income," Peter said. "The government does show up once in a while to give them money, which is almost meaningless. These are people that are living off the land. And they are so happy. I'm sure they have stress. How they're going to eat, or drink, or take care of their families, or get new shoes, meet their basic needs. But these are really pure, happy people. They get up in the morning and they have a smile on their faces. And they're nice to everybody; it's just amazing. Even the old people don't look so old."

So, after Peter's privileged experience, what was his most poignant memory from his thirty-six hours there?

"How happy the kids were," Peter replied. "Every kid had this big, beautiful smile. And the minute they saw me their faces would light up," he said. "I'm talking about kids who had no toys and no TVs. They're running around barefoot, half-naked, playing games with sticks. And they're just laughing and having a great time."

Today, some of these experiences seem to have translated into Peter's own life. "I want my kids to live in the moment, and be appreciative," he said. "At Christmas, Ellen and I took them to this place called the Lydia Home, which is an orphanage for older kids — my kids' age. And these kids come from really, really bad situations. I take my kids there because I want them to see what the real world is all about."

Also part of Peter's "obsession with creating good kids" is to "totally de-emphasize all material possessions in front of my children," he said. "Like a new car is not a big deal, a new shirt's not a big deal. So that these kids don't get obsessed with material possessions." As Peter spoke, it seemed to me that his trade of a watch for a travel experience that turned spiritual still ripples in his life today.

During the weekend between our two-part interview, Peter's five-year-old son, Nicky, who "had no idea that you and I had been talking about this," came to his dad and asked, "Where are your Africa pictures?"

Coincidentally, Peter's wife, Ellen, recently had begun creating photo albums of their years of travels. So, that Saturday, Nicky crawled into bed with his father and they looked at Peter's photographs, again. "He loves looking through the pictures," Peter said. "I think he's interested. He sits and he stares at them, and asks a million questions. And, from reviewing that book, Nicky was obsessed all the next day. He went online to Google Images and made his *own* photo album of animal pictures. And he's already started to ask when he can go to Africa."

As we started to wrap up our interview, Peter grew quiet for a moment. "These experiences, which you're making me think about now, I wonder, *What good are they?* It's sort of selfish to say, 'Well, I just wanted to see the world.' But they taught me valuable lessons," he said. "In fact, it just hit me in the middle of our conversation that the *meaning* of this — the opportunity that I had to go away — is: if I hadn't taken those trips, I know I wouldn't be the person I am today. And I think that is going to end up making me a better parent," Peter said. "And, hopefully, my kids will become better people for it."

Live an Abundant Life

1. *Discover your paths to abundance.* In what area of your life would you like more abundance? The physical, mental, emotional or spiritual? Once you've declared that, pay attention on the road. Signs are often everywhere, paving the way to greater self-actualization.

2. *Practice other "Miller-isms."* Such as, consider all of the ways that you can live "joyously, drunkenly, serenely, divinely aware."

3. *Create an abundance map.* Design a collage of images that suggest an abundant life to you. Then notice over time how aspects of your dream start to manifest in your daily life.

Chapter 9

Kindle the Spirit of Travel, and Life

A S WE TRAVEL SO WE LIVE.
Author Robert Fulghum wrote, "All I really needed to know I learned in kindergarten." I believed that all I really needed to know I had learned from the road, or from others who had traveled there.

I also had often heard dancers say, "We dance as we live." Golfers enjoy a similar analogy. I discovered that we, too, often travel as we live. And like mastering any pursuit in life – golf, dance, writing – I understood that living a richer, fuller life would take continued practice and dedication. It also would require additional approaches, wisdom and expansion. In that spirit, the following pages contain more stories and suggestions from fellow travelers; more life lessons uncovered on the road, more paths to passionate living.

Always Travel with An
Open Mind and a Sense of Humor

George, a wine connoisseur and educator, born in Dalmatia and raised in New Zealand, who lived in the States for many years and now resides in Italy and Tasmania, said:

"A favorite travel moment was the time I thought I was flying to Paris and went to Reykjavik instead," George recalled. "I had to go to France to be admitted into the order of St. Emilion for my work in helping the winemakers of St. Emilion in the American market. There was going to be a High Mass, and I was going to be dubbed on the shoulders with a sword and given a sash. Well, I had to find my own way there, and, one day, walking down Fifth Avenue past Rockefeller Center there was a travel agency that had a special: New York to Paris, $250 round-trip. And I thought, *That's bloody marvelous!*

"So I went in, set the dates, and bought the ticket. And my ticket said, 'New York to Paris.' So, I got to JFK, went to the lounge at the gate, and there was a pedestal with a sign: 'Flight So-and-So: Paris.' So, I got on board. And we'd no sooner leveled off when the pilot came on the P.A. and said, 'Welcome on board, Ladies and Gentleman. It's a pleasure to have you on board this evening. Our flight time to Reykjavik will be…' What?! Where in the hell is Reykjavik? I didn't realize it was in bloody Iceland," George said, giggling.

"Well I got to Reykjavik at four-something in the morning, and the bar was open. The flight to Paris was scheduled for three hours and fifty minutes later, which meant I might miss the train from Paris to Bordeaux. Anyhow, I walked into the bar and I got my first glance of Icelandic women. They were all wearing these huge fur jackets, drinking great cans of beer. And when they finished their cans of beer, they just crumpled the cans with their hands…" George chuckled.

"Anyway, when it was time to get on the flight to Paris, I was in a bit of a panic because I thought I was going to miss my train connection. Well, we couldn't take off immediately because there were sheep on the runway. Yes. And there no was no one to sort of 'shoo' them away. You know, like Meryl Streep in *Out of Africa* said 'Shoo!' to the lion?

"Well, we finally took off and got to Paris, and I got to the station with only a minute left to catch my train. Now the train goes to Portier. Then half the train goes to La Rochelle, and the other half goes to Bordeaux. I'm in this cabin with a Swiss tourist and I'm bushed at this stage, so I fall asleep. The next thing I know, this train has stopped and this fellow is shaking me on my knee to wake me. And I looked, and the train had stopped. *Ah, we're in Portier*, I thought. So I grabbed my bag and we both stood on the platform. It was about 3:20 in the morning.

"So the train moved. And, as we knew, half the train was going to keep going and the other half was going to stop there and take us to Bordeaux. Well guess what? The train kept going, and going. And, suddenly, there was no train anymore. And I'm standing on this platform, in the middle of nowhere, and, of course, the station was closed. There's no stationmaster, there's nothing. Well, there was a phone. And it was a direct line to the stationmaster's house. I spoke with him and he said there was nothing I could do; I had to call a taxi. So I called a taxi, and this sleepy Frenchman came in his pajama pants and a jacket and we had to chase the train. Well, we caught the train, about forty *francs* down the road.

"I got on, got into my cabin, and we took off. And the same guard from before came on, checking tickets again. And he looked at me, did a double-take," George continued, now laughing so hard he could barely finish the sentence, "and said, 'Where the hell have you come from?'

"Well, we finally got to Bordeaux and I had arranged to meet a friend in the station café. And I thought, *Have I got a story to tell him*...This man, a Frenchman who was driving from Montpellier, was also being intronized into the order of St. Emilion. He didn't have a budget for this exercise. But he had a friend in the car business, so he had bought a new car and was going to drive it there and drive it back and do a deal where he gave the car back on his return to Montpellier. Well, he didn't bother to insure it. And, eventually, he showed up and I looked at his face and it was ashen. On his drive from Montpellier to Bordeaux, some kids in the middle of the night were playing on an overpass and dropped a brick on his car, which put a dent in the hood before it broke his windshield. The car that he hadn't insured, of course, because he was giving it back in a few days.

"Well, we had to race to this High Mass," George said, "and I looked like crap at this stage, as you can imagine, and he, poor fellow, needed a stiff drink. So we found this little hotel. Oh, I forgot to mention; my luggage at Reykjavik went on a plane to Stockholm!

"So we found this little hotel. It was a Sunday morning and we said to this fellow at the hotel, 'Oh we just want a room for a half-hour. To clean up, you know.' So the fellow looked at us: *Uh, huh…Two guys…No luggage…And they want a room for a half-hour? Uh, huh…*Oui, monsieur…*Uh, huh…*" George said, giggling again.

"He sold us the room for half an hour," George said. "And we cleaned up and eventually got to St. Emilion to take part in the celebrations."

I have known George for ten years. During this time, he has encountered numerous challenges on a grand scale, including a life-threatening disease and the loss of a limb. Yet as he spoke to me about how he continues to contend with these ordeals today, I realized that his motto for the road, "Always Travel with an Open Mind and a Sense of Humor" also had become a life motto.

Don't Wait

"Don't wait until you have a partner, spouse or a companion to travel with," Loretta, an African American woman, who traveled solo to Tanzania, said. She went to Africa "hoping to get that *Roots* thing," she said, chuckling. She didn't find *Roots*, but, following her other philosophy to "Ask for what you want in life," she'd requested, through a U.S. travel company, to meet the Laibon, the spiritual leader of the Masai tribe, after whom she'd named her American jewelry company. Getting an audience with the tribe's most revered elder, who was also a rituals expert, healer, and diviner, was not an everyday occurrence. And it never would have happened if Loretta hadn't vowed to "take one international trip per year, with or without a companion."

Create Your Travels and Your Life ✍

Although well traveled as a competitive tennis player in her teens, Patsy had only traveled outside the U.S. once when, at nineteen, her mother sent her to Europe. "Don't call home for a year," her mother said. "You can write, but don't call, and don't come home."

Patsy traveled to various European cities seeking a spot she could temporarily call home. Yet she found no place, until Madrid, where, ultimately, she had "the most glorious time of my life," she said. She dated local men, went to bullfights, took flamenco lessons, improved her Spanish, and discovered an artistic bent within herself she had not yet tapped.

Patsy's mother's directive might sound dramatic to many, but, Patsy, now a sixty-something painter, sculptor, realtor, adventurer, wife, and grandmother, said the experience taught her how to "Create a life for yourself." She has encouraged her two children to do the same and today still strives to develop an extended family through good friends — new and old — and loving relationships. And, in any new situation, she always asks herself: *What can I bring to this experience? How can I strengthen it?*

It seems that Patsy's time on the road as a teenager taught her well.

Choose Your Companions with Care ✍

Sheila, a teacher and mother of a young daughter, wrote, "A vacation two hours away can, in many ways, be just as much fun, exciting and life-affirming as a trip to a faraway place, if you are with the right people."

Describing a long weekend reunion in Palm Springs with four

of her closest college girlfriends, she said, "We could have been anywhere. What mattered was all of us spending time together, catching up, reliving past adventures. It helped that we were in a 'vacation spot' and it took me out of my everyday world to spend the day at a spa with cucumbers over my eyes, eating figs…but what stands out for me, above and beyond everything, is how great it was to be with good friends; the energy and support of people you love."

Always Seek to Deepen Your Understanding

"I had no idea what it was going to be like, being a nice Jewish boy living with Catholic people in a nunnery," Bobby said. "Foreign land, no language capabilities, jungle. All of these things were kind of anxiety producing." Just out of medical school, on his first trip outside the States, Bobby traveled to Central America to practice ophthalmology on blind Guatemalans. "It was an incredible experience, living with these people and seeing their rituals," Bobby said. But, on the way home, he got very sick. "I was diagnosed with Shighella, which is like typhoid," he said. "And I vowed then that I would never go out of the country again." Yet Bobby was so moved by this initial trip to Guatemala that, since his recovery from that illness, he has traveled to more than two-dozen countries. And still he seeks to immerse himself in some of the native customs.

"Every time I go somewhere totally different, like Istanbul, I want to go to a religious service," he said. "When I was first in Guatemala, I went to a church service, which was partially Mayan and partially Spanish. And they had all these heavy incense waving candles and the entire place was filled with their fragrance. They use that in Hindu services, too," he said.

"Now at least once on each trip, I will walk into a church, temple, shrine or mosque, and ask if there are any rituals I could watch, or be part of, without upsetting them. Because I know that so many problems in the world today, unfortunately, have to do with religious biases that if you can understand different religions a little better, you can understand why some of these things happen."

Go While You Can

Diane, a woman in her seventies, now battling several debilitating medical conditions, said, "Travel while you still have youthful vigor, good feet, and an open mind. My husband and I never could afford any of the vacations we took, but we went anyway and never regretted a dollar we spent. We still revel in the memories today."

Enjoy the Pleasures of Processing

"For me, there are three stages of the trip," Lucia, a financial planner said. "There's planning the trip, taking the trip, and processing the trip. That is, creating the story and scrapbook afterward. So the end, the scrapbook, even influences the pictures I take on the trip. And as I take pictures, something usually jumps out as a theme. I start to collect anything that's graphically interesting, representative. On a recent trip to France, it was wine; and what bubbled up around that was corkscrews. I took lots of photographs of them, bought every postcard I could find on them, and we ended up collecting a bunch of antique corkscrews from different flea markets. I also keep a journal on the trip — more bullet points," she said. "And I'll make a list of the 'Top Ten': Things I'd do again; things I'd never do again, and funny things that happened," Lucia said. She concluded about her processes, "Any time you do something more consciously it enhances your experience. It just puts you into the mode of observing more carefully."

Although Lucia grew up traveling — her father was an airline pilot so, sometimes, when Lucia wanted to go to the beach, she might travel to Hawaii for the day — she said she had "never thought of any of my travels as being transformational." Until, she told me, "I started with your suggestion of coming up with the 'magic moments' and letting something surface from there. And in the process of searching for the transformation," she said, "I was reminded that I had *experienced* it that way."

On a trip to Ireland with her mother, the two women "had talked about feeling more Irish than we'd ever felt before, even though we'd had a whole lifetime of saying we were Irish. But it was through the process of writing the story," Lucia said, "that it became clear how transformational it really was.

"The extension of this story," Lucia said, "is that two Christmases ago, my mother asked me to make her a tape recording, instead of giving her a gift. For some reason, I just dragged my feet and never did it. Well, it struck me as I was writing this piece for you that I would record this story for my mother. Because she is legally blind now. She can't read. She can't look at scrapbooks. She only has her memories to treasure."

In the End, Have Memories to Show ✍

Donna, a mother of two, said: "I have always loved to travel. As a kid, I loved going on vacation with my parents and would sometimes cry on the plane ride home because I was so sad it was over. My mother used to say that I preferred to live on vacation than in reality, and I think she was right.

"Now that I'm older, I still love to travel and I've been cutting out articles on great hotels, wonderful sights and interesting places for years — I don't always get to see them in person, but my files continue to grow because 'you never know' when you might.

"I keep my love of travel alive by watching the Travel Channel, reading travel magazines and searching Expedia.com for vacations. I think the introduction of web sites, such as Expedia and Travelocity, have enhanced the lives of travel junkies. Whenever I read about a great place, I immediately do a Google search and try to find as much information as I can about that place.

"And I have always said that, at the end of the day, I want nothing to show for my money except memories. I try to pass this on to my kids by not stressing the importance of 'things' but, rather, the importance of experiences."

Keep Seeking the Facets of the Diamond ✍

When I asked Max, a university professor who often guides students on trips abroad, about his most significant travel experience, he said, "Probably the next one. I think that will be my most significant one. You can reflect on ones of the past, but they build up. They are facets of a diamond. And there's always a missing facet, which is your next trip. It's like that diamond with a rough edge that still needs to be polished," he said.

"Charles Eames used to say, 'One of the most important things is to go beyond the point where other people stop, satisfied.' It's asking, what else is there? What else could it be?"

As Max spoke, I realized the same could be said of living richer, fuller, more adventurous lives. If only we could keep asking, keep seeking, *What else is there? What else could it be?*

‿❧‿

For the Road, and Home

Tips to Discover Greater Self-esteem
1) Seek Someone You Admire
2) Choose One Quality You Want More of in Your Life
3) Enjoy a Year of Passionate Living

Tips to Take More Risks
1) Add a Quiet Risk to Your Next Journey
2) Try One New Thing Each Year
3) Explore Your Hometown or State through a New Lens

Tips to Buck Convention, Celebrate Your Individuality
1) Discover What is Essential to You
2) Be Different
3) Draw Outside the Lines

Tips to Slow Down and Live in the Moment
1) Slow Down with a "Sensuality Day"
2) Be a Writer for a Day
3) Develop Your Own "In-the-Moment" Practice

Tips to Connect with the Power of Nature
and Find Your Wild Side

1) Allow Nature to Become a Theme in Your Travels
2) Cultivate the Connection Back Home
3) "Adopt" a Wild Animal

Tips to Feel Sexy

1) Flirt like an Italian, a Cuban or Hemingway
2) Dance, Dance, Dance (or Fish, Fish, Fish)
3) Be an Actor for a Day

Tips to Step into Your Courage

1) Adopt a Local Hero
2) Go Solo
3) Bring Your "Road Courage" Back Home

Tips to Live an Abundant Life

1) Discover Your Paths to Abundance
2) Practice Other "Miller-isms"
3) Create an Abundance Map

Full Collection of Tips

Tips to Discover Greater Self-esteem

1) Seek Someone You Admire

Discover a historic or contemporary figure who has always interested you. Read everything you can about this person: biographies, newspaper articles, web postings, even their letters, if available. In the case of artists, study their work. If this figure was a musician, imbue yourself with his or her music; rent their CDs from the library, or buy them. If the person you admire was an athlete, try their sport. Immerse yourself in the work and life-story of someone you admire.

Next, design your own Footsteps Adventure. Choose a place that was significant to your hero. It may not be their homeland, so look closely. Then travel to that place. Ideally alone, or with a supportive friend, partner or acquaintance who shares your interest. Ask yourself this one question before, during, and after your journey: *What can I learn from this person and their place?*

You do not need to launch a grand overseas adventure, though you may. You could choose to track someone from your home state or town. The key is to immerse yourself in that person's story. Through your study of them, you also will learn about your own life.

The people we are attracted to are often mirrors: glimpses of our desires, shadows of our potential, touchstones for our lives. If we dig deep enough, we can discover the mysteries within ourselves. Perhaps the person possesses a quality that has lain dormant in us; or an attribute that has been quashed in our everyday lives; or a quality we could not imagine ourselves possessing but relish in others. There is a reason we feel attracted to our heroes, and it may not be the obvious one. Dig deep. Explore. Enjoy your journey of discovery.

2) *Choose One Quality You Want More of in Your Life*

Travel can augment your self-esteem because you see yourself in a new light, test your preconceptions, gain a new perspective and feel expanded. Travelers often report liking themselves better when they have traveled because they tapped new aspects of themselves. When we feel greater self-esteem, we feel more passionate about life; and when we like ourselves better, we *like* better, period.

I have highlighted eight qualities for richer, fuller living in the previous chapters, with additional ideas in the section "Kindle the Spirit of Travel, and Life." Which quality do you desire more of in your life? Do you want to be more of a risk-taker? Slow down and live in the moment? Have greater self-esteem? Maybe you want more silence and serenity as a springboard to more fulfilled living. Determine a quality that could help pave your path to a more passionate life, and choose only one.

Then, as you plan your next trip, design one activity that will feed that quality on your journey. If you desire a greater spirit of adventure, plan any event, from skydiving to attending a museum exhibit alone. Whatever feels adventurous to *you*.

Then record your thoughts and feelings before and after the event. Before you go, consider what you hope for. What do you fear? Then go and embrace that activity. Record your reactions as soon as possible afterward, even if you are not able to be in a secluded, quiet place to write. Just write. Write how you felt *during* the experience and how you feel now, just after.

You have just glimpsed your expanded self.

You can apply this exercise to group travel as well. For example, if you seek a stronger spirit of adventure, when the group has free time, take a walk through town alone, instead of napping or spending time with people you already know. Go into the heart of a place. Talk to locals. Browse a neighborhood grocery store. Ask the grocer about local delicacies. Bring a phrase book, if you are in a foreign country, and speak a few words of the native language.

Allow your desired quality to become a theme for your travels. If you seek a greater spirit of adventure, ask locals and fellow travelers what great adventures they have had in their lives. What adventures have inspired them, shaped them? What about the historic figures of the area? Might you emulate experiences they had to develop your adventurous spirit?

Then, back home, recall yourself at the cusp of your adventure: leaping out of the airplane; asking a local person to dance; speaking to a stranger in your first words of a foreign language.

Do you have a photograph of yourself at that moment? At the locals' dance? In the skydiving airplane? Photographs are great mental triggers of our desired states. Hang that picture above your desk at work, or home, or wherever you most desire that quality. If you want to live more in the moment, especially with your children, place the photograph in a room where you often spend time with your family.

Get a clear mental picture of that memory in your mind: the moment when you were on the precipice of expansion, ready to step further into the person you want to be. Use this visual image, and writings and photographs if you have them, to carry that sensation forward. Draw on the scene the next time you need this quality: in a difficult business meeting, a challenging discussion with a partner or friend. This mental snapshot is your touchstone. Reach for it whenever you feel the quality dwindling in your life.

3) Enjoy a Year of Passionate Living

Buy or create your own *Change Your Life Through Travel* ™ workbook. Devote each month of the year to developing a quality that will promote more passionate living. Design your book as you like. You might focus on the qualities you most desire first. Or let the annual calendar inspire you: December could be the month to "Slow Down and Live in the Moment," which could lead into the holiday spirit, or help combat possible pre-holiday stress or blues. Deem February the month to "Feel Sexy," whether you are in a relationship or single. Decide to "Find Your Wild Side" during the spring.

Make the quality a theme for that month. Invite opportunities to exercise it. Read or watch movies about people who embody that trait. Try a new activity related to that quality. For example, during the month when you've decided to "Feel Sexy," try dancing, or another hobby that engages your physical side. Or, to "Find Your Wild Side," visit a wild animal park, zoo, or take a hike in nature. Invite a friend, spouse or partner to join the exercise as well. Engage their creativity about ways to cultivate the characteristic. Have fun with it.

Record your efforts to develop this quality. For example, you might write: "This week I took a risk by…" Then make notes about it. It could have been talking candidly with your partner, jumping on a river raft, or trying a new hobby.

At the end of each week, review what you have accomplished and reward yourself. Passion is a pleasure-seeker and loves rewards. Writing teacher Tom Bird suggests you decide to gift yourself for furthering your goals. Maybe you love chocolate but don't allow yourself to eat it often. Set aside special sweets for this occasion. Or perhaps you'd like an hour to yourself each week. Negotiate, in advance, with your spouse or companion, that you will need an hour alone each week of that month. And if you haven't maintained your commitment to risk that week, return the reward. As passion loves pleasure, you'll find yourself continually cultivating the quality to reap both the short- and long-term rewards.

As you develop your chosen attribute, try also to travel to one new place each month, if only for a day, and if only in your hometown. Your excursion need not be far. Visit a nearby spot you've never explored, or if you don't have time for a longer trip, a park, botanical garden, or museum. Go with a traveler's eye and see what you uncover.

Also, as you map your month-by-month journey to richer, fuller living, consider when you will take a longer trip during that year, like a weeklong holiday. Once you decide your focus quality for that month, it'll add a crackle to your trip preparation and possibly a spark to your travels that you hadn't otherwise anticipated.

Finally, if a monthly commitment sounds too daunting at this stage, extend your workbook over several years. I would not recommend longer than this because it'll be harder to track results and produce sustainable progress. Then watch, review, and revel in your advancement over time.

Tips to Take More Risks ✒

1) Add a Quiet Risk to Your Next Journey

Risk-taking expands us. Enlivens us. Stretches us in ways we were not stretched before. Whatever the results, we are never the same as we were: the moment before we asked, the moment before we danced, the moment before we loved.

Travel provides countless opportunities for quiet risks. Seeking directions from a stranger and allowing them to guide you there. Sampling food you have not tried, then conversing with the chef about it. Traveling alone. Quiet risks that can lead to magic moments are there for the taking. We must just pay attention when they appear, reference our inner maps for safety and then let them guide us there.

Whether in your hometown, or the other side of the world, take one quiet risk on your next journey. You don't need to identify the risk before you depart. Just deem that you will risk and record that commitment in a journal or workbook that you keep for your travels.

When you arrive at your destination, remain open to the nature of your risk. Suggestions often come as gentle whispers, hints hiding in the shadows. Look around corners. Follow the unexpected. Allow your plans to change.

2) Try One New Thing Each Year

My friend, Daune, tries one new activity each year. She has performed stand-up comedy, learned to fly an airplane, attended relationship seminars. Each year she undertakes one new activity that involves risk and growth.

I find participation is key, in almost all situations: the more I participate, the more involved I feel, and the more I then derive from the experience. Rather than sit on the periphery considering what I don't know, I am better when I jump in.

Ideally, combine your new initiative with a destination you wish to visit. Find an activity linked to that area. Drive cattle in Wyoming. Tango dance in Argentina. Explore coral reefs in Australia. View it as a portal to the place. Step through it. You might just find a new passion along the way.

3) Explore Your Hometown or State with a New Lens

Borges found his greatest explorations in his native land. We can too. We can experience our hometown, or home state, differently, if we travel with an open lens.

Go somewhere in your region you've never been. Perhaps you live in the desert but have never visited one of the local lakes. Kayak there. Take a moonlight hike in a nature preserve. Visit a local farm or vineyard. Learn about products produced in your area. Ask if you can help press grapes, or pick fruit. Get involved.

Take a museum tour. Ask questions. Talk to a curator. Introduce yourself to another person visiting the museum. Ask what they like, or don't like, about the exhibit. Then consider how you felt when introducing yourself to a stranger, and perhaps experiencing some of their interest or insights into the art. Could you feel positive about taking that "quiet risk," whatever the result?

I remember my parents creating similar excursions. While raising my brother, sister and me in a suburb of Chicago, my mom and dad would take each other on "mystery dates." One would surprise the other for a day, or an evening, and they would explore a place or activity they hadn't tried before. During one of these mystery dates, my father helped fly a hot air balloon in rural Illinois and later earned his pilot's license. My mother learned how to dance the Texas Two-Step and drink long-neck beers at a cowboy bar on Chicago's west side.

Kate, who traveled in Captain Cook's path, said, "We used to do this thing when I worked at the Phoenix Art Museum. We called it the Friday Afternoon Club. Several of the design and curatorial staff would take turns on Fridays taking our fellow workers to someplace in downtown Phoenix that we hadn't discovered. We'd all pile into a car and go to some crusty, old, funky 1920s junk shop, or a used bookstore, or a really authentic restaurant on the west side where a goat was roasting on a spit in the backyard." One of the joys of this experience, Kate said, was to "get out of the museum and into our town and be kids again."

Find a way to see your homeland differently. You'll appreciate your surroundings more and perhaps even see yourself differently in the process.

Tips to Buck Convention, Celebrate Your Individuality ✤

1) Discover What is Essential to You

As Karen Blixen suggested, determine what is essential to you. Is it freedom? Family? Art? Political ideals? Look to your travels for clues. Blixen discovered freedom was key to her. Others have found friendship, or family, as essentials on the road. Look in your journeys for signs of yourself and, when you discover landmarks, return to them.

2) Be Different

Travel provides prime opportunities to act differently. The moment you travel, you have broken your pattern, your routine, left your quotidian; and, in the process, pried open a gate to other possible departures.

So, on a future journey, experiment with a less predictable way of being. Step outside your normal behavior. It might just remind you that it is okay to move beyond boundaries we often create in our everyday lives.

3) Draw Outside the Lines

My parents used to like telling a story of when I was in third grade. I had finished my work in the classroom, and quietly walked to a corner of the room and stood on my head. Whatever prompted this, I have no idea. But I didn't worry that kids would think I didn't know how to be "normal." And I understood that normal didn't constitute standing on my head in class. But it made me feel good. I could see things differently from that perspective.

I enjoy hearing this story retold as an adult because it reminds me that sometimes in life we just need to "stand on our heads."

How about drawing outside the lines? Do you remember how good it once felt to draw outside the lines? How about getting up every morning, for a week, a month, or more and drawing? Draw a big square in the middle of the page, with thick, bold borders. Then design a way outside those lines. Cut across them. Draw around them. Circle them. Grab different colors. Draw wildly, around, inside, and out of those strong, dark lines. Add a splash of color, sensation, whimsy, as you create bursts of energy, color, *passion* outside those lines.

Then go back. What did you want to be when you were a child, when you were alone in your room at night? Who did you want to be? Where did you go when you fantasized? What did you do when you colored outside the lines?

Have you touched that childhood dream? If not, consider it now; and think how, everyday, you can continue to draw outside that box in your daily life and re-connect with that child who once, boldly, drew outside the lines.

Tips to Slow Down and Live in the Moment ✍

1) Slow Down with a "Sensuality Day"

Declare one day a month as a "Sensuality Day." Devote an afternoon or an evening, if a full day is impossible. Take a bubble bath. Listen to your favorite classical or jazz CDs. Feel the firmness of your bed, and the weight of the sheets on you. Delight in everyday household tasks, as D.H. Lawrence did. Cook a leisurely dinner. Enjoy the warm, soapy water as you, slowly, wash dishes.

Set part of your Sensuality Day outdoors, if at all possible. Create an afternoon picnic or a sunrise gathering. Bring elements that represent sensuality for you: food you love, good wine, music, a cherished book, friends you enjoy, a treasured article of clothing, stories to share. Bring a reading that inspires you, that reminds you that life is richer than we often know. Maybe it is something you have written; a travel recollection that enlightened or expanded you. Or a poem by a writer such as Walt Whitman, Rumi, or Maya Angelou. Seek recommendations from friends, librarians. Preparation for your Sensuality Day also can help perpetuate the spirit of sensuality in your everyday life.

Stage this experience monthly, if possible. Otherwise, dream of it and repeat it whenever you need more sensuality: more slowing down and savoring in your life.

2) Be a Writer for a Day

According to travel and nature writing professor Paul, a key to successful writing is to fully immerse yourself in a scene. Look for telling characteristics about people. Listen for overheard dialogue. Focus on all of your senses, one at a time. Discover new ways of describing what you experience. What do you see? What do these images remind you of? How does the experience shift when you employ a new sense? Create analogies for your sensory experiences. Wordsmith. Draw comparisons between tastes, smells, sounds and the feel of things. Let the words become paints on a palette. Live like a writer for a day.

If you are traveling with a friend, I suggest you encourage him or her to participate as well. Describe senses you are experiencing to each other. Compare notes. Resist discussing, "What's next?" in your travels, or what's passed. Stay in the moment —in that Tuscan kitchen, with the sights, sounds, smells, tastes and opportunities for touch. Ask to feel the pasta dough, help to roll it. The more actively you engage each sense, the more enhanced your experience and memory of that moment will be.

Max, the university professor who often leads trips abroad, said, "When I travel with students, I give them an exercise where they just have to go out and observe things. They have to write about them; that is, describe them with a narrative. They also need to draw them by hand: to really slow the eye, connect the hand, and draw things, *before* they ever take a photo. They take a moment to pause and study something and digest it."

Finally, to step into a writer's shoes, be curious. Even if you do not feel interested in a situation, *pretend you are.* You can jump-start your curiosity by simply engaging fully in the experience. Psychologists have described how couples with marital problems can *pretend* they are happy, even when they are not. With time and dedication, they often wake up weeks later genuinely happier in their relationship. This can work with curiosity as well. It is like smiling when you feel depressed. It's very hard to do.

Be curious about all of your surroundings. Ask questions. Recall wonder. If you don't speak the language, seek out someone who does. Engage an interpreter. Curiosity feeds curiosity. The more you have, the more you want. Savor this benign drug, this benevolent addiction.

I realized that all of the literary heroes I tracked shared this fervent curiosity. No doubt it nourished their craft and fueled more passionate lives.

3) Develop Your Own "In-the-Moment" Practice

Mark, who traveled to the British Virgin Islands, meditates. Gloria, who made annual trips to Iran, takes new routes when she runs errands. Others I interviewed swim, golf, journal, practice yoga, make pottery.

I walk every morning. I live on the shores of a manmade lake in Arizona and now, every spring, I notice when the birds' bare winter song has grown full, their liquid lyrics float in the dry desert air. The mourning doves coo their melody, like notes on a wooden recorder. Mallards tap their beaks at the surface of the pond, like an ancient sewing machine. I feel the morning sun on my arms. Pick a sprig from a rosemary bush. Move through my senses as I would in a foreign land: in the kitchen of an Italian chef, ambling through the African bush.

When I lose the moment, or have trouble finding it, I reconnect by asking: *What one new thing can I notice today?* Soon, the frenzy of thought that had fragmented me has quieted. And I am back, in the moment.

How will you practice? What will you create that will serve as a daily reminder to savor slowing down and living in the moment?

Tips to Connect with the Power of Nature and Find Your Wild Side ❧

1) Allow Nature To Become a Theme in Your Travels

"Living in a natural state." "Not cultivated, tamed, domesticated." These rank among the definitions of wild. It is what is inherent to us, what is intrinsic: our most elemental instincts.

In nature, we can shed our outer layers. Feel unfettered, free, pure. When we touch this state we feel *good:* our most essential, authentic selves. Connected to our baser beings, our surroundings, we are receptive, attentive, attuned and, at times, ecstatic. We feel calm, pure of spirit, powerful, engaged, present — whole.

Nature invites us to shuck our often complex and complicated lives and trappings and return to a more primitive state, return to ourselves.

Abbey would urge us to get into nature as much as possible.

And if you can't walk, sit. Dave, a retired art teacher, who has been described as "a man who lives to love nature" once told a student: "Go into nature and sit for one hour. Watch the light change. Watch it as it moves through the trees. You will learn as much about yourself in that hour as you will learn about nature."

Allow nature to become a theme in your travels. I've driven cattle for a week in Wyoming and slept under the stars for seven nights. I have mountain trekked for four days to reach Machu Picchu, instead of riding the train. These explorations can provide powerful entry points to places you are visiting, portals to places you will come to know. And you might just unearth an aspect of your wild side along the way that you did not know you had.

2) Cultivate the Connection Back Home

Paul, the travel and nature writing professor, suggests that people select one spot in nature and go there for a half-hour every week. It can be a park, a mountain preserve, a garden, your backyard. Record your observations of that place and your experiences in it.

After following in Ed Abbey's footsteps and practicing Paul's exercise back home, now each day as I stroll beside my nearby lake, I wonder what fresh surprises will await me. Will the newborn rabbit let me step closer today than it did the day before, as it nibbles on grass? Will the Great Blue Heron, with a fishing line caught in its mouth, let me walk nearer, in my impossible desire to help? Will the hummingbirds let me stand beside them as they feed? Will the ducks eat grain from my hand?

In your chosen place, ask yourself: *What emotions does this place evoke? What makes me smile, feel good, or feel sad here? What intrigues me? What memories can I carry back into my daily life that can continue to delight and serve as a touchstone of my connection to nature?*

Barbi, who hiked in the Grand Canyon, and who also seeks to cultivate her connection back home, suggests, "We need to create opportunities to pause and connect to things larger than ourselves. We need the pause. The pause allows us to connect to what's greater than us. And that's where our power comes from: whatever that is for *you*.'

"It's easier in nature," she says, because "there aren't so many layers of information. There isn't so much clutter that gets in the way. The Buddhists talk about the quiet, empty mind, and that is something I bring back with me, the need to find that empty space as much as I can, day-to-day.

"For me it's how I start my day," Barbi said. "It's tapping into that quiet every morning. When I swim in the morning it's very quiet, even though I am swimming with other people at a club. It's so quiet because all you hear is your own breathing and the water moving. I meditate when I swim. It's being quiet and listening. Really listening to everything that comes in.

"Or walking home from teaching last night the moon was up. And I thought, *Thank you, moon.* When I see the moon up in the sky like that — especially one of those big old moons — I try to draw a triangle between me to the moon to someone I want to connect with. I think, *They're seeing the same moon that I'm seeing!* So it's like this connection, which is comforting to me. It's a form of connection to people I really love.

"It's about getting down to what really matters, and about being reminded of what we need to feel whole," Barbi said. "And when I lack that piece, or those pieces have been scattered out on the deck some way, how do I begin to pull them back to me? I know I can reconstruct it. It's knowing that you can tap into it whenever you want, and you've got to be clear enough to do that. It's there; it's always there. We don't have to go to nature...but I think we need to sometimes, to remember."

3) "Adopt" a Wild Animal

If you have a pet, your animal can offer clues.

Your animal rushes outdoors and rolls in the grass or dirt.

When was the last time you flopped on a stack of leaves? Or romped in the snow on a winter's day?

The spontaneous spurts of spirit we see in our domestic animals can spark our own wild side. Like small shafts of light in our portals to more passionate living.

Determine a wild animal that has always interested you. Perhaps it is a dolphin, a butterfly, a lion, a whale or hawk; or a gorilla, as Glenn discovered. Choose an animal that has always appealed to you, if only in a passing way. Decide to learn about that animal. Read about it, online and off. Make the animal a focus of a future trip, or of a visit to the local zoo. Watch animal documentaries on television. Sponsor an animal online. You can do this through various organizations, where you pay a fee and the company will send you updates about "your" animal's life and progress.

Post a picture of the animal that interests you in your office or home. Allow it to be an ongoing symbol of your connection to your wild side and a suggestion of an attribute, or attributes, that you would like to continue to cultivate. Can you adopt aspects of the animal's behavior? Walk proud like a lion? Swim for hours in the sea like a dolphin? If you have chosen a hawk, would you like to learn to fly? Ask what you can discover from your chosen animal. What qualities does it command that you might desire in your life, or that you already possess but have not fully adopted? What shadow parts of yourself does this animal represent, and might help evoke, in you?

Tips to Feel Sexy ✑

1) Flirt Like an Italian, a Cuban or Hemingway

Wouldn't it be great to move through the world "flirting with" more people and animals? Imagine: no agenda, no objective, save the joy of engagement and interaction.

Spend an afternoon this way. You may pass many people and not connect with them. But when you do, if only with a fleeting glance on the street, that moment can be magic. As Melissa, who traveled alone in Italy for a month, suggested, it is a life force. And the true joy is that you don't know how much you may also have sparked someone else's day. Sometimes an unexpected human connection can make another person feel vibrantly alive.

Discover who you can meet, who you can talk to. Arnold Samuelson, a young American writer who spent time with Hemingway in Havana, said that Papa met people in Cuba by talking with them at hotels, in line at cafeterias. Follow Hemingway's lead. Engage a range of people. Surprise yourself.

2) Dance, Dance, Dance (or Fish, Fish, Fish)

Throw yourself wholeheartedly into an interest. Maybe it is something that has always intrigued you but you've never explored. Studies have even proven that couples in long-term relationships can rekindle excitement in their relationship by trying challenging or new hobbies together. Follow that which you've always been curious about. Interest often provides a clue to passion, and pursuing it might enliven you in ways you have never imagined.

Have you ever found yourself attracted to someone who is not at all "classically" beautiful or handsome but is wildly attractive? Years ago I knew an academic whose dear friend described him as "one of the homeliest men I've ever met." Yet the professor swarmed with admirers, male and female, of various ages, because he was so *passionate* about his subject. His ebullience became a beacon for others.

I love dance because it engages all of the senses — touch, sight, sound, smell, even taste, as sweat trickles across my lips. This engagement of all the senses helps to fuel a sense of sensuality for me. Whether I am dancing alone in my living room or with a partner on the floor.

Sexiness is, partly, an ease and presence within your body. Many women have described other ways they have found to strengthen this connection. For some it is yoga, hiking, even a rigorous game of tennis. Of course I believe an ideal hobby is one that also provides travel opportunities. Women I spoke with have traveled to Japan, Italy, and Mexico on yoga retreats, learning about the local culture as they experienced a favorite pastime.

Feeling sexy is like using a muscle. If we don't use it, it will wither. Your sensuality offers a way to feel more centered, joyful, powerful. Admire it. Exercise it. Flex it.

3) Be an Actor for a Day

Back home, sometimes I would walk as the Cuban women did. Most often, I would walk this way alone. This was not about sex, romance, or courtship: it was about feeling sexy *inside*.

Discover the local ways of flirting in a foreign land. Maybe it is the open, honest pollination Melissa observed in Italy. Or the surreptitious glances we sometimes see in Middle Eastern countries. Or the way the Cubans seem to wear their sensuality on their skin. Study how people move their hands, hold their heads, walk, smile. Practice their gestures; move with the pace and precision of their walk. Be an actor for a day.

Then, back home or on the road, consider: who do you find sexy? Who has an allure that captivates you? Maybe it is a movie star, sports celebrity or a political figure. Ask yourself what makes them sexy *to you*. Answer this and you will discover as much about what you may lack or desire in yourself as you will about the person you admire.

Tips to Step into Your Courage ✍

1) Adopt a Local Hero

Consider ways to ingratiate yourself into a local culture. Learn as much as you can about a place before departing. Read books by local authors, past and present. Study the area's history. Research the local customs, and once a door opens to you in a local culture, step through it. Use your internal compass to guide you in how far to go. Follow your inner maps. Then allow your experience to unfold. If invited, visit a native's home. Stay for that extra cup of coffee. Go to the local dance. Follow the thread. Let the tapestry of your experience grow.

I have found that, particularly when I talk with local people about historic figures of their area, many open up as they might not otherwise. They know I care enough about their culture to have researched some of its lesser-known aspects. In turn, they seem more inclined to share some of their gifts with me.

Adopt a local courage hero. Allow it to become a conversation-starter with local people. Ask who they deem to be courageous Italians, Australians, Russians, Swedes, Americans, Norwegians. Who do they admire in their country's history?

Explain that you would like to learn more about their culture. If you don't speak the native language, go to an office of tourism, or a big hotel where staff are likely to speak English. Talk to people there.

Pretend you are a television interviewer. Employ the "5 W's." Ask: Who? What? When? Where? Why? Learn as much as possible about the local culture from the native people.

Once home, look up the hero on the web or in your local library. It'll be a way to extend the power of your journey — to the place and to yourself, once back home.

2) Go Solo

Traveling alone can kindle your courage. If you have a spouse, partner or friend you often travel with, seek a pardon, if only once. While traveling with companions can provide wonderful opportunities to share the joys of travel, solo travel can be a very different experience: requiring different faculties, different coping mechanisms and sometimes even a different outlook.

Traveling alone can offer great rewards. First, you automatically test your courage as you may not when traveling with others. Emotions such as loneliness, or questions of self-sufficiency, also can arise that might not otherwise. Second, you often experience the *place* differently. You are more inclined to reach out, talk to people, and your opportunities to integrate yourself into a culture notably expand.

3) Bring Your "Road Courage" Back Home

The PBS General Manager who suggested I read Borges told me that my solo travels were like being able to star in my own movie. We can all star in our own road movies. Yet, like good actors, we must study a part and then *become* it.

Earlier, I described ways to fully experience and record memorable moments in our travels. Now it is time to process and integrate those experiences.

Getting back onto a horse after falling when I was in New Mexico might not feel particularly courageous to veteran horse owners or frequent riders, but it *felt courageous to me,* and that is what matters. Finding those moments when we must tap the courage that arguably already exists within us. *That* becomes our act of courage. The act that can buoy us; thrust us out of our sometimes dulled or dampened existence.

I liked the way I felt the week after I returned from Mabel Dodge Luhan's New Mexico. I reveled in it. To keep that spirit alive I would revisit my trip journal, recalling, vividly, the sensations, as I rode into the barn, with the smell of hay in the air, the sweat on my skin, the heat of sun on my face, the sting in my bottom where I had fallen against cactus.

I would play that scene over in my mind of my small, personal victory, and don a bracelet I had bought from the owner of the trading post; now another symbol of courage that I'd tote on days when I felt I might need more of it.

What was a moment when you felt courageous? Maybe it is one you have yet to create in your future travels.

Next time you journey, seek to create such a moment. Then, back home, ask yourself several questions: Why was this experience significant? What quality, or qualities, did you discover or further tap into? What was it about the experience that helped you recognize that quality? What have you done to process your experience back home: shared stories with friends? Reviewed your journal? Created a photo album? Stayed in touch with people you met on your trip? Written travel stories? Finally, how have you maintained this quality in your everyday life?

Michael, who cliff dove in Jamaica, said it took time for his realization to arise. That is, he didn't immediately convert his Jamaican memory to an understanding of how to take more calculated risks. He learned that later, after processing the experience back home. How did he do that?

First, he recognized the importance of opening himself to such experiences. "As humans, we learn most when we get out of our comfort zones," Michael said. "But it's antithetical to the body's premise of trying to stay in a state of relaxation and comfort. And it requires purposely fighting off mechanisms that exist within us — whether in our minds or our bodies — the inclination to stay comfortable, to stay in the known, to stay in the certainty of predictability."

Second, Michael adopted the ritual of recording his experiences. He likes journaling, but you can create a photographic journal if you are more visual. As digital cameras have made photography easier and more cost effective, you can keep a personal journal through pictures, if you prefer it to writing. Create what my nephew, Joe, calls "Memories in Media," or if you are writing,

"Adventures on Paper."

Finally, Michael proposes revisiting these memories, time and again. "Journal your experience and what you learned from it. Then come back to it, again and again. Re-read that passage about what you experienced, what you felt, what you learned, and how you have incorporated that into your life. The practice of writing and reading something helps jog our memories; puts us in that moment again. If we do that often enough, then we begin to see the world through the eyes of that experience. And we become more aware when something similar occurs so that we can react in a similar way, and use what we learned."

Tips to Live an Abundant Life

1) Discover Your Paths to Abundance

Imagine imbuing your days, your weeks, with passion. Miller found sex, travel, conversation and letter-writing as paths to passion. What are yours?

Before you set out on your next trip, decide one area of your life where you'd like more abundance: more richness, bounty. Is it the physical, mental, emotional or spiritual? Maybe you want richer relationships. Or more love, like Ellen created in her path. Or you may want more challenging work, or to learn a new skill that will bring you pleasure.

Your travels can offer opportunities to explore alternate vocations and avocations. Be a grape picker, shadow an airplane pilot, a brewmaster, or a TV producer. Sometimes you can create these experiences on your own, or you can travel with a company that organizes such experiences.

Whatever you want, in whichever quadrant of your life, declare it clearly and write it down. Then, on the road, *pay attention*. Employ your imagination. Signs are everywhere. When you have a focus you look at people, places and events through a new lens.

Enjoy this invitation to open yourself to new ways of seeing, new ways of being.

2) Practice Other "Miller-isms"

Determine all of the ways that you can, off and on the road:

- Pay attention. As Henry Miller said, "The aim of life is to live, and to live means to be aware, joyously, drunkenly, serenely, divinely aware."

- Expect everything, and be "ready to give everything," as Miller would say. Contribute.

- Relish "the divinity of man." As Rochelle and Jeremy discovered, acknowledge, enjoy and celebrate the "divinity of man" (and woman).

3) Create an Abundance Map

Spend a rainy, blustery or sweltering summer afternoon, or a lazy Sunday, creating a collage. Go through old magazines and stacks of unsorted photographs. Tear out and set aside images that appeal to you. Don't over-think them. Just quickly cull pictures that grab you. It could be a photograph of your fantasy car; children playing on the beach; symbols of a loving, intimate relationship; places you dream of visiting; pictures that evoke a sense of serenity and peace or of how to make the world a better place. Whatever suggests an abundant life to *you*. They can, but need not, cover each of the physical, mental, emotional, and spiritual quadrants of your life.

Include symbols of abundance from your life today. What are you grateful for? Author Jack Canfield says, in *The Success Principles,* "When you are in a state of appreciation and gratitude, you are in a state of abundance...Your focus is on what you have received, and you always get more of what you focus on."

Have fun with this project. Play favorite music while you cut and paste. Mount the images on cardboard however your imagination dictates. Then hang it in a place of prominence, perhaps over your desk at home, work, or in a corner of your kitchen, if cooking or healthy eating form part of your abundant life picture.

Enjoy your creation. See it as a representation, and map, to your life's abundance. Look at it often and notice over time how aspects of your dream start to manifest in your daily life.

Several years ago, I created my own abundance map. Every image represented a goal, dream or something I felt grateful for and desired more of in my life, like travel. Six years later, while writing this book, I discovered that I had realized all of those glossy dreams.

If journeying through life with a traveler's lens can help fulfill your dreams of a richer, fuller, more adventurous life, why not start packing your suitcases with memories now?

⚕

Afterword

To luggage — *By Patricia Cherin*

I always have at the ready
big suitcases, behemoth containers
with empty insides
valises not yet predisposed

it started I remember
in the ninth grade
when I got matched Samsonite
for Christmas: blue vaults with gold clips

I still buy always the biggest suitcase on display
such greed of the heart
to think one can take one's stuff
for comfort, decoration, venal transcendence

many pilgrimages are done
the Algonquin, the Café Dome
the boathouse at Laugherne
but the perfect lover still may come

and, of course, there's the rest home
someday I will pack them
one last time, place them by the door:
grand crammed carpetbags

(how vain to think mine only will have THAT bow)
I need to think they will be with me
at the final passage, on the great Grand Tour,
there for the big trip

Notes/Reading List

MY ODYSSEY BEGAN IN BOOKS and continued on the road. I have not attempted here to list all of the books that influenced me on this journey, as that would require more space than I have available. But I did want to mention key sources that I referenced and enjoyed during my travels.

Introduction

"Song of the Open Road" by Walt Whitman. For those who like to hit the road or journey from their armchair, Whitman delivers timeless inspiration.

Discover Greater Self-esteem &
Buck Convention, Celebrate Your Individuality

Isak Dinesen: The Life of a Storyteller by Judith Thurman. Director Sydney Pollack says this book and Thurman's extensive knowledge of Blixen's life, along with Dinesen's *Out of Africa* and other writings, formed the chief background sources to make the film *Out of Africa*. The best biography I have read on Blixen.

Letters from Africa: 1914 – 1931 by Isak Dinesen. Blixen's letters provide a more visceral depiction of her Africa experiences than *Out of Africa* and *Shadows on the Grass*. Great for anyone interested in learning more about the writer's African experiences.

Take More Risks

Borges: A Life by James Woodall. Woodall makes a smart, accessible guide to Borges's life and work.

Slow Down and Live in the Moment

The Letters of D.H. Lawrence by D.H. Lawrence. Lawrence was a prolific writer and these letters provide some of the undistilled impressions that would later form a foundation for his travel narratives.

D.H. Lawrence in Italy by Leo Hamalian. An informative biography of Lawrence's experiences in Italy. Hamalian visits most of Lawrence's old haunts and depicts the writer's life there.

Connect with the Power of Nature and Find Your Wild Side

Adventures with Ed by Jack Loeffler. Loeffler's self-described "biographical memoir" is an illuminating romp through Loeffler's friendship with Abbey and provides insight into the writer's life as only a fellow "desert rat" could.

Edward Abbey: A Life by James M. Cahalan. An excellent, very thorough biography.

Confessions of a Barbarian: Selections from the Journals of Edward Abbey, 1951 – 1989, edited and introduced by Dave Petersen with illustrations by Abbey. For those who consider Abbey merely a "barbarian," these journal writings prove otherwise. They reveal his passion in his youth, optimism, and desire to live fully — abundantly, as Henry Miller would say.

Feel Sexy

Hemingway in Cuba by Norberto Fuentes, with an introduction by Gabriel Garcia Marquez. A valuable resource for anyone interested in Hemingway's life in Cuba.

The Faces of Hemingway: Intimate Portraits of Ernest Hemingway by Those Who Knew Him by Denis Brian. Brian talked with a range of people who knew Papa, which resulted in this rounded portrait of the man.

Step into Your Courage

Mabel Dodge Luhan: New Woman, New Worlds by Lois Palken Rudnick. A wonderful exploration of the complex life and transformation of Mabel Dodge Luhan.

Winter in Taos by Mabel Dodge Luhan. My favorite Dodge Luhan memoir in which she transports the reader into her life in Taos.

Lorenzo in Taos by Mabel Dodge Luhan. Another look at Mabel Dodge Luhan's Taos life, highlighting her relationship with D.H. Lawrence and the years he lived there.

Live an Abundant Life

The Colossus of Maroussi by Henry Miller. Miller's pivotal journey through Greece and probe into the soul of the place.

A Literate Passion: Letters of Anais Nin and Henry Miller 1932 – 1953 edited by Gunther Stuhlmann. A collection of letters between these two long-time friends, lovers and colleagues.

The Devil at Large by Erica Jong. An excellent exploration of Miller's life and work by Jong, who knew Miller and was befriended and lauded by the famous author.

The Success Principles by Jack Canfield. Packed with useful information, inspiration, and valuable guidance, this is a great resource for entrepreneurs or people seeking to take their lives and work to the next level.

Television programs/videos:

Images of Arizona by KAET/Phoenix. An intimate journey to some of Arizona's most magnificent destinations through the eyes of three celebrated photographers.

Rite of Passage: Mabel Dodge Luhan by KNME/Albuquerque.

An informative documentary focusing on Dodge Luhan's life in New Mexico, including interviews with people who knew her there.

Additional travel writings/evocations of the chosen places by their historic writers:

Out of Africa and *Shadows on the Grass* by Isak Dinesen. Lyrical evocations of Blixen's life in Kenya and memories of her adopted homeland from back in her native Denmark.

Twilight in Italy, *Etruscan Places*, and *Sea and Sardinia* by D.H. Lawrence. Lawrence's three travel books set in Italy.

Down the River by Ed Abbey. A collection of Abbey's essays, including his narrative on Aravaipa Canyon.

Edge of Taos Desert: An Escape to Reality by Mabel Dodge Luhan. An account of Luhan's first few months in New Mexico.

The Old Man and the Sea by Ernest Hemingway. Hemingway's famous fish tale set in Cuba, which precipitated the author's winning the Nobel Prize in 1954.

Islands in the Stream by Ernest Hemingway. Published posthumously and set partly in Cuba, many consider this to be Hemingway's most autobiographical work.

❧

Acknowledgments

THIS BOOK, like every other major project in my life, is the result of a tremendous team effort. I extend my deepest appreciation and gratitude to:

My mother, Gloria, my tireless editor, for all of her long days, unwavering dedication, and editorial wisdom. My father, Bill, for being the best champion and business advisor I could ever ask for. I could not have done it without both of you. Thank you. My brother, Randy, my sister, Kerry, and my nephews, Jack and Joe, for their promotion, proofreading, and brainstorming contributions. My brother-in-law, Bob, for his business advice early on. And my partner, Jim, for his endless support and love along this journey.

My wonderful colleagues and friends who took time out of their busy schedules to read and review this book on short notice: Laura Gross, Leigh Flayton and Adam Davis, as well as Paul Morris, for his great mentorship over the years, and Melissa Pritchard, who contributed a beautiful story in this book as well. *All* of your early editorial insights and keen feedback helped to make this a better book.

My designer, Peri Poloni-Gabriel, for her outstanding work and for being much more than a designer. My copy editor, Janice Phelps, who remained steadfast with this manuscript to the end. Richard Maack, who contributed valuable guidance on the interior photographs. And Win Holden, Kim Ensenberger, and Bob Albano, for their publishing advice en route.

Robert Kiyosaki, Cyndi Simon, Harvey Gammage, Sandra Etherton, and Michael Lechter, who provided sound business advice when I needed it. Jerry Simmons, Sharon Crain, Liz Dawn, Ariel Wolfe, Michael Dixon, David Weiner, Doug Corcoran, Gayle Shanks, Greg Giczi, Kelly McCullough, Jack Canfield, and Veronica Romero, for their promotion ideas and assistance. As well as Michael Harris and David Eichler, for their marketing suggestions and thought-provoking interviews for the book.

Bruce Covill, for his incredible support over the years and his web site partnership. And Jack Sullivan, for his design creativity for the web site and beyond.

Dr. Paul Coulombe and Carol Rhoades, who helped keep me healthy as I journeyed around the world.

Shelley Rodrigo Blanchard and Michelle Hammers, who provided initial research for my writers' journeys. Suzanne Guery for her dynamic contributions from the project's infancy. Jason Covill for his administrative and research help during production. And my friends at Channel 8, who supported me when I wanted to follow a dream.

Barbara Fenzl, Sharon Lamm, Michelle Wynne Johns, and Daune Finke, for their continuous friendship as I have traveled down this path. And Terry Walker, for his exhilarating guidance along this open road.

Tom Bird, who inspired me to write a book in ninety days. I

didn't quite make ninety, but he showed me what was possible. And Dan Poynter, whose invaluable book on publishing made this an exciting, and much easier, journey.

And, most of all, the following people who provided interviews or wrote to me about their life-enriching travel experiences. Even though, unfortunately, I was unable to include all of your stories, every one of you helped to shape this book as well as how I think, and feel, about travel's indelible power to change lives. Thank you for your passion, insight, wonderful tales, and wisdom, without which this book would not have been possible:

Jeremy Adair, Lisa Barron, Harriet Bernstein, Steve Birenberg, Jeanette Booker, Jane Burtnett, Barbi Crisp, Patricia Cherin, Roz Childe, Billy Cioffi, Joe Dean, "Mo" Dean, Laura Distelheim, Rochelle Distelheim, Carrie Demont, Jack Dykinga, Sheila Farr, Jerry Feldman, Gloria Felice, Glenn Felner, Koji Fujita, Craig Garfinkle, Donna Grace, Randy Gengarelly, John Haas, Howard Haas, Lucy Herrman, Dave Hetrick, Gwen Hillis, Loretta Love Huff, Alex Johnson, Diane Kopp, Peter Kupferberg, Hugh Lambert, Margene Lambert, Dave Lash, Bobby Lewis, Michael Lofquist, Patsy Lowry, Alan Maites, Joe Manning, Shannon Mishkin, James Makau Nzioka, Mark Peters, Lucia Renshaw, Renee Rivers, Hilly Rose, Jean Rincon, Jim Ryder, Carol Schatt, Don Schultz, Theresa Shedric, Maire Simington, Marty Snitzer, David Sparks, Ellen Stewart, Vicki Stouffer, Gustavo Tapia, Erleen Tilton, Kate Timmerman, Wylie Timmerman, George Truby, Tony Sutcliffe, Max Underwood, Jan Wood, and John Woodin. You all are the stars. Thank you for allowing me to help you shine.

Share with Us

I HOPE THIS BOOK has helped pave your path to richer, fuller and more adventurous living. If you would like to share your tales of transformative travel, or your reactions to stories or suggestions in this book, please visit **www.footstepsadventures.com**

Or write to: Footsteps Media
#621
6929 N. Hayden Rd. Ste. C4
Scottsdale, AZ 85250

Also, to learn more about life-changing travel and the Change Your Life Through Travel™ Charitable Partnership, please visit www.footstepsadventures.com. The Change Your Life Through Travel™ Charitable Partnership supports organizations that provide grants for travel that can change lives. A percentage of the proceeds from sales of this book will go to that cause because we believe that if we seek magic in our travels, we can find it, just as we can find it within ourselves.

www.footstepsadventures.com